MW00770390

TO:

....

FROM:

....

DATE:

....

The
Pray Better
Devotional

The
Pray Better
Devotional

Meditations for Women

PLUS
BONUS
PRAYER MAPS!

Donna K. Maltese

BARBOUR
PUBLISHING

Published by Barbour Books, an imprint of Barbour Publishing, Inc., 1810 Barbour Drive, Uhrichsville, Ohio 44683, www.barbourbooks.com

Our mission is to inspire the world with the life-changing message of the Bible.

Member of the
Evangelical Christian
Publishers Association

Printed in China.

THE SECRET OF WHO

*He who dwells in the secret place of the Most High
shall remain stable and fixed under the shadow of the
Almighty [Whose power no foe can withstand]. I will say
of the Lord, He is my Refuge and my Fortress, my God;
on Him I lean and rely, and in Him I [confidently] trust!*
PSALM 91:1–2 AMPC

When it comes to prayer, there are at least two parties: God and you. God is the One who is almighty. He's the Most High, the One whose "power no foe can withstand." You're the one who is to make God your safe place. It's in Him you live, move, and have your being. While you're abiding in God 24-7, allowing Him to shield you, protect you, and watch over you, no evil can touch you.

Today, imagine yourself living in that "secret place," the one reserved for God and you alone. Trust that the God in whom you abide is bigger than any problem or challenge you may face today or tomorrow.

*Lord Most High, I come to You in the most secret of places,
the one You and I share alone. Shield me, Lord, from all danger.
Keep me close and safe as I lean on You and trust in You. Amen.*

THE SECRET OF WHAT

One of His disciples said to Him, Lord, teach us to pray, [just] as John
taught his disciples. And He said to them, When you pray, say: Our
Father Who is in heaven, hallowed be Your name, Your kingdom come.
Your will be done [held holy and revered] on earth as it is in heaven.
LUKE 11:1–2 AMPC

Jesus knew the power of prayer, how it rewards and transforms
the petitioner (you) and moves into action both you and God. Both
Matthew (6:9–13) and Luke (11:2–4) recorded Jesus' outline of prayer,
the one you are to follow when you go before the One whose "power
no foe can withstand" (Psalm 91:1 AMPC), whether that foe is earthly
or supernatural.

Today, seek your reward, transformation, and inspiration by
taking up the unique privilege and power of prayer. Begin by simply
folding your hands and saying, "Our Father in heaven, hallowed be
Your name. . . ."

"Our Father in heaven, hallowed be your name. Your
kingdom come, your will be done, on earth as it is in heaven.
Give us this day our daily bread, and forgive us our debts,
as we also have forgiven our debtors. And lead us not into
temptation, but deliver us from evil" (Matthew 6:9–13 ESV).

THE SECRET OF WHEN

He then told them a parable on the need for them to pray always and not become discouraged. . . . "Will not God grant justice to His elect who cry out to Him day and night? Will He delay to help them?"
LUKE 18:1, 7 HCSB

Can you imagine baking a cake without a spatula, knitting without needles, scrapbooking without scissors, or driving a car without brakes? Just as every worker in every trade or task needs certain tools to do her job, every Christian should be using the privilege of prayer to live her life in God's will and way. Prayer is the most powerful tool you have. It's not to be neglected, nor left in the rain to rust. It's to be used every moment of every day. For the more it's used, the more powerful both you and it become!

Today consider the requests—both old and new—you've been bringing before God in the past few weeks. Which ones have you perhaps given up on? Consider bringing them back to God, expecting Him to answer you in His time.

Help me, Lord, to pray always, not to get discouraged but to come continually to You with my requests, knowing You will answer in Your time. Amen.

THE SECRET OF WHERE

When you pray, go into your [most] private room, and,
closing the door, pray to your Father, Who is in secret; and your
Father, Who sees in secret, will reward you in the open.
MATTHEW 6:6 AMPC

In His Sermon on the Mount, Jesus gives instructions for what to do and what not to do when it comes to prayer. He begins by telling you not to be like the hypocrites who love to pray in public so they may be seen by and win the admiration of others. Instead, you're to go into your most secret place, close the door, and secretly talk to Father God.

Where's your secret place or "prayer closet"? If you don't have one, consider creating one. Find an area where you might be able to spend a few minutes focused and undisturbed each day. Bring a Bible and paper and pen with you, but leave the phone behind. If necessary, put up a DO NOT DISTURB sign, mentally and physically, so others will know you're not to be interrupted. Then pray, knowing that as you do so in secret, God will reward you in the open.

I want and need some undisturbed one-on-one time alone with
You, Lord. Show me where that secret place might be. Amen.

BURDEN BEARER

Blessed be the Lord, Who bears our burdens and carries us day by day, even the God Who is our salvation! Selah [pause, and calmly think of that]! God is to us a God of deliverances and salvation; and to God the Lord belongs escape from death [setting us free].
PSALM 68:19–20 AMPC

You have an awesome God. Who else but He would offer to bear your burdens? In fact, He doesn't just volunteer to carry your load of worries. He *insists* upon it! And His help doesn't end there. God doesn't just insist on carrying your burdens. He wants to carry you as well! Why? Because that's who God is: the burden bearer—just one more reason to begin your day praising Him.

Today, as you pray, imagine God as your Shepherd. See Him not just taking care of you—protecting, nourishing, and calming—but actually *gathering* you up in His arms, carrying you "close to His heart. . .gentle in leading those that are with young" (Isaiah 40:11 NLV).

Dear God of gods, I'm unable to stand beneath the weight of my worries and woes. But You can carry anything. So I allow them to slide off my shoulders and am free. Praises to You, the One who carries me day by day! Amen.

REALITY CHECK

Elijah said. . ."I've been working my heart out for GOD, the GOD-of-the-Angel-Armies, because the people of Israel have. . .murdered your prophets. I'm the only one left, and now they're trying to kill me."
1 KINGS 19:14 MSG

Working through the prophet Elijah, God had displayed publicly His awesome power, then He'd seen to the annihilation of hundreds of false prophets (1 Kings 18). But afterward, fear struck Elijah's heart as Queen Jezebel threatened his life, prompting him to run away into the wilderness. When God asked him, "What are you doing here?" (1 Kings 19:13 MSG), Elijah made it sound as if he were the only prophet left! But God knew the true case. So He redirected Elijah, telling him to go back the way he'd come and anoint two new kings and another prophet (19:15–16).

God expects and commands you to pour out your heart to Him. But He'll also ask you to reconsider any assumptions that might be misleading you or triggering your worries. For only when you know the reality of where you are will you truly see and hear God's redirection.

Today, when God asks, "What are you doing here?" truthfully reconsider your problems, then leave the real troubles at His feet.

Lord, here's what I'm worried about. . . .

GET AWAY

"Are you tired? Worn out? Burned out on religion? Come to me. Get away with me and you'll recover your life. I'll show you how to take a real rest. Walk with me and work with me— watch how I do it. Learn the unforced rhythms of grace."

MATTHEW 11:28–29 MSG

God knows you need His help. That there will be times when you get burned out, times when you suddenly realize you've been trying to live life on your terms, through your own energy and strength, instead of on God's terms and with His power.

God knows the rest you need. That's why He wants you to come to Him and take a load off, to get away with Him. Only then will you be able to recover your real life, take a true rest, and refresh your heart and soul. Only then will you have the freedom to walk and work with Jesus, to be as He is, do as He does.

Today is your day to recover your life. To get back on track in your spiritual life. To get away with God and find His rest awaiting you.

I'm coming to You, Lord. Show me how to take a real rest in You. Amen.

GOD SEES

When they came near the city gate, a dead man was being carried out. He was the only son of a woman whose husband had died. Many people of the city were with her. When the Lord saw her, He had loving-pity for her and said, "Do not cry."

LUKE 7:12–13 NLV

One of the greatest things about Jesus is that He truly *does* care about you. For no one has more love or compassion for you than He. Jesus, your Friend, Brother, and Savior, knows you inside out. He knows where you've been, where you're going, and what's happening in your life in this very moment.

When Jesus saw a widow sobbing over the loss of her son, He knew what emotional, relational, and economic hardships awaited her. Acting out of love and compassion, before she even *asked* for help, Jesus raised her son from death and returned him to his mother.

Today, realize that God sees you. He knows all that's going on in your life. Chances are, before you even brought your concerns to Him in prayer, He already acted with compassion on your behalf. Imagine what more He'll do when you lay your troubles at His feet.

Have compassion on me, Lord, as I lift my concerns to You. Amen.

YOUR SHEPHERD

The Lord is my Shepherd [to feed, guide, and shield me],
I shall not lack. He makes me lie down in [fresh, tender] green
pastures; He leads me beside the still and restful waters.

PSALM 23:1–2 AMPC

God is your Shepherd. And as your Shepherd, He promises to provide for you. It is God who will and does feed your body and your soul. But He doesn't stop there. God is the Shepherd who will guide and direct you, showing you where He would have you go and what He would have you do. And like any good shepherd, God also protects you from anyone and anything that may attempt to harm you.

Because your Shepherd is also the Creator and Sustainer of the universe, you'll want for nothing. If there's something you need or desire that He wants you to have, have it you will.

Today, heartfully acknowledge God as your Shepherd. Allow Him to lead you to green pastures and beside still waters so that you will have all the tranquility you need.

You, Lord God, are my Shepherd. Because You are with me and
in me, I know I will never lack for anything. You are the One
who makes me lie down in soft, fresh green pastures. You are
the One who leads me to still and soothing waters. Amen.

27

RENOVATION AND RESTORATION

He refreshes and restores my life (my self); He leads me in the paths of righteousness [uprightness and right standing with Him—not for my earning it, but] for His name's sake.

PSALM 23:3 AMPC

There may be times in life when you are so busy working and taking care of others that you lose yourself, the woman you are, the one God created you to be. That's when you need to sink yourself deep into God, realizing and acknowledging that it is He alone who can refresh and restore you to yourself. He alone will watch over you, cuddle you, strengthen you, and ease your mind and heart while you take a breather.

Once you've caught your breath, allow God to lead you where He will. Don't try to resist His guidance. Instead, be as pliable as you can while He sends you down the right road. Remember, God has plans for you, plans to prosper you, not to harm you. Thus, you can trust Him to lead you the right way.

Thank You, Lord, for restoring me to myself, giving me the refreshment I need. Lead me down the right path, the one on which I can best serve You. In Jesus' name, amen.

SHADOW WALKERS

Yes, though I walk through the [deep, sunless] valley of the shadow of death, I will fear or dread no evil, for You are with me; Your rod [to protect] and Your staff [to guide], they comfort me.

PSALM 23:4 AMPC

The world can be a dangerous place. Evil can lurk in the shadowy darkness. Yet even though that's where you may be walking, you need not fear or dread. Because God, that great and good Shepherd who loves and leads you like no other, is with you.

No matter what or who is trying to frighten you by planting threats or seeds of worry in your mind, take no account of them. Do not listen to those voices. Instead, remember God (aka, your Good Shepherd) and think on His words. Remember the tools He carries. He has His rod to protect you, to fend off whatever evil or trouble comes your way. And He has His staff as well, to guide you and give you comfort.

Today, as you walk amid the shadows, remember the Light who walks with you. With Him by your side, you need not fear or dread *anything*! Simply believe.

Because You're with me, oh Lord, I need not fear nor dread anything. For Your rod protects and Your staff guides. In and through You, I have all the comfort, shielding, and direction I need. Amen.

BLESSINGS AWAIT

You prepare a table before me in the presence of my enemies.
You anoint my head with oil; my [brimming] cup runs over.
PSALM 23:5 AMPC

. . . .

Jesus isn't just your Good Shepherd. He's also your friend, your traveling companion, and your host. In the valley of the shadow of death, God has a table waiting for you. For you He has prepared the tastiest morsels. While your powerless enemies look on, God is serving you a banquet of fine food and drink.

God is also looking to refresh you, His guest, by pouring oil on your head. Meanwhile, your cup of wonderful water or wine is brimming over.

Suffice it to say that God, your Shepherd, has all your blessings already waiting for you. All you need to do is seek His presence, follow His guidance, believe in His love and protection, and sit down at His feast. He's done it all for you.

Lord, as I come to You, into Your presence, I find all the
blessings You have waiting for me. As my enemies, now
powerless, look on, I enjoy the feast You've provided.
Refresh me, revive me, renew me. In Jesus' name, amen.

STEPPING OUT

"Moses my servant is dead. Now therefore arise, go over this Jordan,
you and all this people, into the land that I am giving to them,
to the people of Israel. Every place that the sole of your foot will
tread upon I have given to you, just as I promised to Moses."
JOSHUA 1:2–3 ESV

. . . .

Imagine losing a vibrant leader, a person you've journeyed with for forty years. Now imagine you are called by God to replace that leader. Would you have the strength and courage to move into the position God has been training you for and has now provided for you?

That's where Joshua found himself after Moses died (Joshua 1:1). And that's when Joshua received his instructions from God: Cross the Jordan and bring God's people into the Promised Land. To reassure His servant even further, God tells Joshua He has provided the territory. But that means nothing if Joshua doesn't step out in faith and *take* the offered territory.

It's the same with you. God has provided you with so many things. But to have those things, you need to step out in faith and take them. Today, prayerfully consider what blessing God has given you that you've yet to take. Then take it!

You've blessed me in so many different ways, Lord. Yet what
blessing still lies before me that You would have me take up?

JUST AS

"From the wilderness and this Lebanon as far as the great river, the river Euphrates, all the land of the Hittites to the Great Sea toward the going down of the sun shall be your territory. No man shall be able to stand before you all the days of your life. Just as I was with Moses, so I will be with you. I will not leave you or forsake you."

JOSHUA 1:4–5 ESV

. . . .

God loves specifics. Here He gives a few to Joshua, letting him know exactly what blessings He has carved out for His people.

God then tells Joshua that no man will be able to stand before him all the days of his life. Why? Because just as He was with Moses, God will now be with Joshua.

What God promised Joshua, He promises you. In this very moment, God stands with you. And because He does so, no one will be able to stand against you. Ever. Why? Because God will never leave you or let you down. Just as God was always with Moses and Joshua, He'll always be with you.

Today, pray that God would plant those truths firmly in your mind and heart.

Just as You were with Moses and Joshua, Lord,
You are now with me, blessing me, leading me, and
standing with me. It's You I serve and praise. Amen.

NO TURNS

"Be strong and courageous, for you shall cause this people to inherit the land that I swore to their fathers to give them. Only be strong and very courageous, being careful to do according to all the law that Moses my servant commanded you. Do not turn from it to the right hand or to the left, that you may have good success wherever you go."
JOSHUA 1:6–7 ESV

It takes a lot of courage to step out in faith, especially when you know you'll be up against some obstacles. For Joshua, those obstacles were enemy armies, city walls, and flooding waters. So God continued to build up Joshua, telling him he needed to be strong and courageous. For that's what the Israelites needed him to be to see God's promise to them fulfilled.

Yet there is a caveat in these words of encouragement from God the Father. Joshua is to be careful that he abides by the law of Moses. *Only if he stays in line with Moses' law* will Joshua have good success wherever he goes.

The same is true for you. You too may be up against some obstacles in your life. If so, pray for God to bless you with strength and courage as you follow the Lord's command to love.

Lord, give me the strength and courage I need to answer Your call and live in Your love. Amen.

MEDITATION

"This Book of the Law shall not depart from your mouth, but you shall meditate on it day and night, so that you may be careful to do according to all that is written in it. For then you will make your way prosperous, and then you will have good success."
JOSHUA 1:8 ESV

God has revealed Himself, His plan, and His purpose for you in His Word. And it is that same Word that will form and transform both you and your world.

Yet for God's Word to be so life-changing, you are to read, study, and meditate on it, not just once or twice a week but day and night! Then you'll understand God's Book better and be better able to obey and act on it. Then you'll get to where God would have you go and be the woman God created you to be.

Today, choose one chapter of scripture to read. After reading it, mark or write out the verse that spoke most to your heart. Meditate on that verse, asking God what He would have you learn and know about it. Make note of where God leads.

Show me, Lord, what You would have me discover, learn, and plant in my heart today.

NO WOES

"Have I not commanded you? Be strong and courageous. Do not be frightened, and do not be dismayed, for the LORD your God is with you wherever you go."
JOSHUA 1:9 ESV

Three times God tells Joshua to be "strong and courageous" (Joshua 1:6, 7, 9). God's repeating of these words means they're important and that all listeners and readers need to be paying attention.

God has *commanded* you to be strong and courageous. Not frightened. Not dismayed. Not discouraged. Not dissuaded. Because God is with you. No matter the time or place, He is by your side.

The beauty of God's words of strength and courage and of His presence is that their effect is contagious. After God spoke all these encouraging words, Joshua shared God's game plan with the Israelites. And their response to him was that they would do what he asked. Then they turned around and encouraged Joshua, saying, "Only may the LORD your God be with you. . . . Only be strong and courageous" (Joshua 1:17–18 ESV).

Today keep in your heart and mind God's command to be strong and courageous.

Lord, only in You and with You do I find my strength and courage. Help me do so today, Lord, as I walk with You. Amen.

→ DATE:

Dear Heavenly Father, ...

....

....

....

....

Thank You for. . ...
....
....
....
....
....
....
....
....

I am worried about. . ...
....
....
....
....
....
....

PEOPLE I AM PRAYING FOR TODAY. . ...
....
....
....
....
....

Here's what's happening in my life. . .

_____

_____

_____

_____

I need. . .

_____

_____

_____

_____

_____

_____

_____

_____

_____

_____

_____

_____

_____

_____

_____

OTHER THINGS ON MY HEART THAT
I NEED TO SHARE WITH YOU, GOD. . .

_____

_____

_____

_____

_____

_____

_____

_____

amen.
Thank You, Father,
for hearing my prayers.

Arrow Power

The king said to me, "What are you asking for?" So I prayed to the God of heaven. And I said to the king, "If it pleases the king, and if your servant has found favor in your eyes, send me to Judah."
NEHEMIAH 2:4–5 NLV

There are times in life when a short prayer, also known as an "arrow prayer," is the best and most efficient tool in a believer's toolbox. One of the most well-known arrow prayers is that of Nehemiah.

Nehemiah, a Jew, was a cupbearer—a wine and food taster—for King Artaxerxes in Persia. As a servant of the king, Nehemiah could not be anything *but* cheerful when before Artaxerxes. Yet how could he be? For he, Nehemiah, had recently learned that the walls of his beloved Jerusalem lay in ruins and her gates were broken. When he first heard the news, Nehemiah wept and prayed. Then he decided to request permission from the king to go to Jerusalem and help rebuild the walls.

When Artaxerxes saw Nehemiah's face and asked why he looked so sad, Nehemiah became frightened. Then, in faith, he plowed ahead, saying, "Why should my face not be sad when the city, the place of my fathers' graves, lies waste and its gates destroyed by fire?" (Nehemiah 2:3 NLV). When the king then asked Nehemiah what he actually wanted, Nehemiah sent up a quick arrow prayer to God before answering his sovereign.

Although it's uncertain exactly what need or desire Nehemiah prayed for, one thing is certain. His arrow prayer met its mark and was answered by God. Have yours?

SERVANT SPEAK

*Samuel went and lay down in his place. The LORD came,
stood there, and called as before, "Samuel, Samuel!" Samuel
responded, "Speak, for Your servant is listening."*

1 SAMUEL 3:9–10 HCSB

. . . .

Three times God called Samuel. And three times the boy ran to the priest Eli, saying, "Here I am; you called me" (1 Samuel 3:5 HCSB). When Eli finally realized God was the One who was really calling Samuel, he told the boy to "go and lie down. If He calls you, say, 'Speak, LORD, for Your servant is listening'" (3:9 HCSB).

Samuel obeyed. When the Lord came and stood before him and said, "Samuel, Samuel!" Samuel responded, "Speak, for Your servant is listening." And God spoke!

God waits for His servants to quiet themselves down, to be alert for His presence, awaiting His words. When you're in a place of silence, within and without, expect God to meet you there, to call your name, to share His plans. Your job is to respond to His call simply and prayerfully with these short yet power-filled words: "Speak, Lord, for Your servant is listening."

*As I come before You today, Lord, in the silence of
this time and place, in Your presence I pray and
say, "Speak, Lord. Your servant is listening."*

HEARTFELT ARROW

Jabez called out to the God of Israel: "If only You would bless me, extend my border, let Your hand be with me, and keep me from harm, so that I will not cause any pain." And God granted his request.

1 CHRONICLES 4:10 HCSB

Not much is known about Jabez, a descendant of David from the tribe of Judah. The only other information about him is from 1 Chronicles 4:9 (HCSB): "Jabez was more honorable than his brothers. His mother named him Jabez and said, 'I gave birth to him in pain.'"

A painful labor is not a great beginning for mother or child. But naming the child "Pain" (or Jabez in Hebrew) was bound to make things even more difficult for him. Yet Jabez was known as being "more honorable than his brothers." Perhaps the moniker "Pain" influenced Jabez's behavior and choices, making him a more honest and upright individual than his brothers.

Regardless of the effects of Jabez's naming, at some point he sent a heartfelt arrow prayer to God, asking for His blessing, more land, His hand to be with him, and protection. Twenty-eight words. And God answered his prayer.

What specific, heartfelt, twenty-eight-word prayer would you like to shoot up to God?

If only You would bless me, expand my prospects, walk with me, and protect me so that evil will not harm me! In Jesus' name I pray. Amen.

AN ARROW BLESSING

*The LORD bless you and keep you; the LORD make his face
to shine upon you and be gracious to you; the LORD lift
up his countenance upon you and give you peace.*

NUMBERS 6:24–26 ESV

For over three thousand years, this arrow-blessing prayer—spoken by God to Moses for Aaron to use—has been making hearts warm, faces smile, and spirits take flight. These words from Numbers have been blessing not just the one who hears them but also the one who speaks them.

God wants you to know He's blessing you! And that He does so not just by giving you things you've asked for in prayer but by giving you things you've *never* asked for or dreamed of! Things you didn't even know you needed!

God also wants you to know He is constantly watching over you. He is beaming His Son-light upon you. And He'll do all He can for you.

And last but not least, God wants you to know He favors you with many things, most importantly, His gift of peace.

Today bless someone with an arrow blessing, knowing that as you do so, you too will be blessed.

*"GOD bless you and keep you, GOD smile on you and gift you, GOD look
you full in the face and make you prosper" (Numbers 6:24–26 MSG).*

45

SHORT, SWEET, AND SPECIFIC

After this, David asked the Lord, "Should I go up to one of the cities of Judah?" And the Lord said to him, "Go up." So David said, "Where should I go?" And He said, "To Hebron." So David went up there.

2 SAMUEL 2:1–2 NLV

David, the boy shepherd who became a king, wasn't perfect by any stretch of the imagination. But he was one of the most loyal and obedient God followers there ever was. Why? Because he trusted God to always be there, listen, guide, and bless. And he knew where to go when he needed wisdom, direction, and love: to God. And once there, David knew what to get: details.

King Saul had been chasing David around for years. And now David learned that Saul was dead. The first thing David did was sing a song of lament. The second thing was to ask God what he should do, where he should go. Although we are not told how long it took for David to get an answer, we *are* told that God did answer—and David obeyed.

Today, consider asking God a specific question (or two). When you receive an answer, offer up a follow-up question. Record where God takes you in this short, sweet, and specific encounter with Him.

Lord, tell me, should I. . . ?

AN AMAZING ARRAY FOR YOUR QUIVER

*I lift up my soul to You, O Lord. O my God, I trust in You. Do not
let me be ashamed. Do not let those who fight against me win.*

PSALM 25:1–2 NLV

. . . .

One of the best sources of arrow prayers is the Psalms. There you
will find an amazing array of short and specific prayers you can use
to suit any and every occasion.

Here are a few for your consideration:

- O my God, I trust in You. Do not let me be ashamed.
  (Psalm 25:2 NLV)
- O Lord, forgive my sin, even as big as it is. (Psalm 25:11
  NLV)
- Turn to me and show me Your loving-kindness. For I am
  alone and in trouble. (Psalm 25:16 NLV)
- Keep me safe, Lord, and set me free. (Psalm 25:20 NLV)

Today, find a Bible translation that nourishes your spirit. Within
those pages, find a psalm that truly speaks to your heart. Within that
psalm, mine the verse, sentence, phrase, or word that pulls you out of
yourself and into God. Then prayerfully bring that heartfelt passage
or word of gold to God. Finally, wait in the stillness, in the silence,
to see what God reveals.

*Lord, "let what is good and what is right keep me safe,
because I wait for You" (Psalm 25:21 NLV).*

→ DATE:

Dear Heavenly Father, ...

....

....

....

....

Thank You for. . . ..

....

....

....

....

....

....

....

I am worried about. . . ..

....

....

....

....

....

PEOPLE I AM PRAYING FOR TODAY. . . ..

....

....

....

....

....

Here's what's happening in my life. . .

I need. . .

OTHER THINGS ON MY HEART THAT
I NEED TO SHARE WITH YOU, GOD. . .

Amen.
Thank You, Father,
for hearing my prayers.

Persistence in Prayer

Be cheerful no matter what; pray all the time; thank
God no matter what happens. This is the way God
wants you who belong to Christ Jesus to live.
1 THESSALONIANS 5:16–18 MSG

Jesus wants His followers "to pray and not to turn coward (faint, lose heart, and give up)" (Luke 18:1 AMPC). For Jesus knows what humans are like. (He was one Himself, after all.) Jesus knows most people will give up praying for a particular happening, a particular outcome, or a particular someone if they don't see a result or an answer from God right away. And because every soul is different, everyone's "right away" is different. It could mean a day, a week, a month, a year, or a decade of the same prayer or request until, seemingly with no answer in sight, a particular request just peters out.

Jesus doesn't want you to give up, lose heart, or get discouraged in your prayer life. Nor does the apostle Paul, who advises you to pray all the time. To thank God no matter what answer He gives you—because His answer, His way, is always the best. Paul also writes, "Pray hard and long. Pray for your brothers and sisters. Keep your eyes open. Keep each other's spirits up so that no one falls behind or drops out" (Ephesians 6:18 MSG).

This week, stick with it—practice persistence in prayer and see how it pays off!

LOOK TOWARD THE SEA

Elijah, for instance, human just like us, prayed hard that it wouldn't rain, and it didn't—not a drop for three and a half years. Then he prayed that it would rain, and it did.

JAMES 5:17–18 MSG

A prophet serving God in the days of kings, Elijah, prompted by God, announced a coming drought to King Ahab, saying, "As surely as GOD lives. . .the next years are going to see a total drought—not a drop of dew or rain unless I say otherwise" (1 Kings 17:1 MSG).

A few years later, God sent Elijah back to tell Ahab He'd be sending rain. So back Elijah went. To the top of Carmel. There he bowed to the ground, put his face between his knees, and told his servant, "Go up now and look toward the sea." The servant did. Seven times he returned to his master's side saying, "There is nothing"; and seven times, Elijah instructed his servant, "Go again" (1 Kings 18:43 NLV). That seventh time God answered, for the servant returned to say, "I see a cloud as small as a man's hand coming up from the sea" (1 Kings 18:44 NLV).

Make me an overcomer in prayer, Lord. Bless me with the faith, persistence, patience, and prayer power of Elijah.

JUST AS BEFORE

When Daniel learned that the document had been signed, he went into his house. . . . Three times a day he got down on his knees, prayed, and gave thanks to his God, just as he had done before.

DANIEL 6:10 HCSB

Daniel was a nobleman taken from Judah to serve foreign kings. Because of his wisdom and skills in dream interpretation, Daniel quickly rose through the ranks.

Eventually, Daniel was the main man put in charge of King Darius's kingdom. That's when other high-ranking kingdom officials tried to uncover anything Daniel may have done wrong in the past. Having found nothing from the past to accuse him of, they came up with a plot to malign him in the present and destroy his future. They suggested the king sign an edict making it unlawful for people to pray to anyone other than the king.

Amazingly enough, that law didn't stop Daniel from praying to God three times a day, for Daniel's prayer routine was an integral part of his life. So he prayed. And that's how he landed in and survived the lions' den.

Today, look at your own prayer routine and consider what has become a mainstay in your own process. What works? What doesn't?

Show me, Lord, how to make my prayer routine an integral part of my life.

52

QUICK HELPER

"Will not God make the things that are right come to His chosen people who cry day and night to Him? Will He wait a long time to help them? I tell you, He will be quick to help them."

LUKE 18:7–8 NLV

. . . .

To help people understand why they should always pray and not be discouraged, Jesus told His listeners a parable.

There was a judge and a widow. The judge thought nothing of God and cared nothing about people. The widow, lowly and unprotected, had no one to go to court for her, to speak on her behalf. So she was forced to stand and speak up for herself. Time after time, she came into court, telling the judge she was being abused of her rights and demanding protection. But he wouldn't even give her the time of day. Still, she kept on coming, stating her case, demanding action. Finally, the judge, worn out from her complaining, made sure she got justice.

Jesus' takeaway was that if this crooked judge would bring about justice for a persistent widow, imagine how much more a loving God will do for you, His dear child!

Thank You, Lord, for being my willing helper and protector. In You alone, my hope remains.

53

THOUGHTS ON THOUGHTS

*"My thoughts are not your thoughts, and My ways are
not your ways," says the Lord. "For as the heavens are
higher than the earth, so are My ways higher than your
ways, and My thoughts than your thoughts."*

ISAIAH 55:8–9 NLV

Face it. Although you're made in God's image, your thoughts have
a mind of their own. Often the things you're pondering aren't even
close to what God has in mind for you, because His thoughts and
ways are vastly higher than your thoughts and ways.

This is where persistence in prayer plays a very interesting role.
For the more you pray about something, the more God refines your
thoughts, making them more and more like His own—until one day,
you understand how to refine your prayers, revise your plans, or
transform your thoughts and ways. You figure out what you really
should be praying for, which turns out to be something that matches
your desire with what God desires for you.

Today, consider your thoughts, desires, and petitions before
God. Ask Him to revise your musings and ways so they match up
with His. Then listen for what *He* has to say, and write down what
and how He'd have you pray.

*Align my thoughts with Yours, Lord.
What would You have me pray?*

FERVENT PRAYER

Peter was kept in prison, but fervent prayer for him
was persistently made to God by the church.

ACTS 12:5 AMPC

King Herod was on a roll. He'd already had John's brother James killed. Now he'd had Peter arrested and put in prison. Yet regardless of King Herod's efforts, there was one thing he hadn't counted on: the power of fervent and persistent prayer.

While Peter was in prison, the believers in "the house of Mary the mother of John, whose surname was Mark" (Acts 12:12 AMPC), were praying for him. Because of their prayers, God sent an angel to light up Peter's cell and wake him up. As Peter rose, his chains fell off his hands. The angel told Peter to get his coat and shoes on and follow him out of the prison and the gates. Before he fully realized what was happening, Peter was in front of Mary's house alive and unfettered.

Today, consider who or what you and other believers might pray for together, fervently and persistently. Who needs your prayers so that they can find their way to freedom in Christ?

Lord, who needs prayers for the help,
power, strength, and freedom found only in You?

→ DATE:

Dear Heavenly Father, ...

....

....

....

....

Thank You for. . . ..

....

....

....

....

....

....

....

....

I am worried about. . . ..

....

....

....

....

....

PEOPLE I AM PRAYING FOR TODAY. . . ..

....

....

....

....

....

Here's what's happening in my life. . .

I need. . .

OTHER THINGS ON MY HEART THAT
I NEED TO SHARE WITH YOU, GOD. . .

amen.
Thank You, Father,
for hearing my prayers.

Jesus' Prayer Perspective and Practices

Now Jesus was praying in a certain place, and when he finished, one of his disciples said to him, "Lord, teach us to pray, as John taught his disciples." And he said to them, "When you pray, say. . ."

LUKE 11:1–2 ESV

Who better to ask how to pray than Jesus? After all, He was God in human form. He'd know the exact approach to use to get God's attention, to curry His favor, to partake in His presence, love, and light, and to make difficult requests. Along with Jesus' knowledge around those aspects of prayer, He would also know the who, what, when, where, why, and how of praying to God.

Jesus, the One in whose steps we are to walk, has left us wonderful guidelines, a clear path, and numerous examples of the practice and power of prayer. For if anybody was a righteous person—someone whose prayer "makes tremendous power available [dynamic in its working]" (James 5:16 AMPC)—certainly Jesus was.

This week's focus will be on Jesus' perspective on and practices of prayer. Here you'll discover why Jesus stepped away to pray and how He made prayer a priority, used different prayers for different occasions, tapped into the power of thanksgiving, and prayed in accordance with God's will. Ready? Let's go!

STEP AWAY AND PRAY

He often withdrew to deserted places and prayed.
LUKE 5:16 HCSB

When Jesus physically walked this earth, time and time again He would regularly step away—withdraw from the world, from the people, from the preaching, teaching, and healing—and pray. Even though the crowds of people and their demands for Jesus' time and healing power kept on increasing, He continued to meet their needs. And the way He did so was by refueling Himself and His power in His time alone with God in prayer.

When removing Himself from the people and demands filling His day, Jesus prayed in gardens (Gethsemane), on mountains, in the wilderness, and in deserted places. Since He taught His followers to pray in closets (Matthew 6:6), Jesus must have prayed indoors as well.

Where do you go when you need some time alone with God? Inside or outside? Up on a mountain or down in a valley? In your room or on the roof? Practice praying in different places this week. Designate the place most conducive to connecting with your Creator as your new place of prayer.

I need time alone with You, Lord, to renew and refresh myself.
From the world I withdraw. To You I lift my voice. Amen.

MAKING PRAYER A PRIORITY

*He made the disciples get into the boat and go
before him to the other side, while he dismissed the
crowds. And after he had dismissed the crowds, he
went up on the mountain by himself to pray.*

MATTHEW 14:22–23 ESV

There were times when even the Son of God had to be proactive in making sure He got some alone time with Father God. . . .

After hearing John the Baptist had been beheaded by Herod, Jesus "withdrew from there by boat to a remote place to be alone" (Matthew 14:13 HCSB). But the crowds still followed Him. When He reached the shore and saw all the people looking for help, He felt sorry for them and began to heal the sick.

Before they knew it, it was dinner time and the people needed to be fed in this remote place. There Jesus worked a miracle so that He could feed the five thousand–plus crowd. After everyone had eaten and the leftovers had been gathered, Jesus insisted the disciples head out on the water while He went up on the mountain *alone* to pray.

Just like Jesus, you too need to make spending time alone with Father God a priority. How can you do that today?

Help me, Lord, to make time alone with You a must today. Amen.

THE LONG AND SHORT OF IT

One day Jesus went up on a mountain to
pray. He prayed all night to God.
LUKE 6:12 NLV

. . . .

Different occasions call for different prayers.

In today's scripture, Jesus spent an entire night on a mountain praying to God. Why? Because His next day was going to be overflowing with challenges. Jesus was going to be choosing His twelve disciples. He'd definitely need a clear head from Father God to make those decisions. Then, after selecting His twelve and coming off the mountaintop, Jesus would be preaching radical ideas to nobodies, prostitutes, sinners, lepers, those troubled by unclean spirits or physical maladies, and religious scholars trying to trip Him up. He obviously needed all the prayer and time in God's presence that He could get.

Although there's no telling how many words Jesus used when He prayed all night, we do know the length of Jesus' shortest *recorded* prayer: "Father, into your hands I commit my spirit!" (Luke 23:46 ESV). It's only eight words long! Conversely, the prayer He taught His disciples—the Lord's Prayer (Matthew 6:9–13)—is sixty-six words long.

The long and the short of it is that it doesn't matter how many words you use in prayer. Just pray as the Spirit leads, knowing God hears.

Immerse me in Your love, Lord. Surround me with Your peace. Amen.

KNOWING THE POWER OF THANKSGIVING

Jesus. . .took the five loaves of bread and two fish. He looked up to heaven and gave thanks. He broke the loaves in pieces and gave them to His followers. The followers gave them to the people. They all ate and were filled.
MATTHEW 14:18–20 NLV

Jesus had spent most of His day healing people. When evening set in, the disciples asked Jesus to send away the five thousand men (plus women and children) so they could go into town and buy food for themselves. But Jesus told His disciples to give the people something to eat instead of sending them away. After His followers concluded that all they had to feed the crowd was five loaves of bread and two fish, Jesus directed them to bring their meager supply to Him.

Knowing the power of gratitude, Jesus looked up to heaven, thanked God for what He had, broke the loaves into pieces, then gave the disciples the food to distribute. After everyone had eaten, twelve baskets of leftovers were gathered.

Today, thank God for the little you have, knowing He'll multiply it as needed.

Jesus, thank You for all You've blessed me with. Please multiply the meager provisions I've put in Your care. Amen.

62

ALL PLANS IN GOD'S HANDS

Going a little farther, He threw Himself upon the ground on His face and prayed saying, My Father, if it is possible, let this cup pass away from Me; nevertheless, not what I will [not what I desire], but as You will and desire.
MATTHEW 26:39 AMPC

Three times Jesus approached God *alone* in the garden of Gethsemane. The first time He threw Himself facedown upon the earth and spoke to Father God, asking Him, if possible, to take away the cup before Him. Yet at the same time, Jesus prayed, "Nevertheless, not what I will [not what I desire], but as You will and desire." He then made the same request two more times, "using the same words" (Matthew 26:44 AMPC).

Jesus was well aware of the truth that God is in charge—that all must be done according to God's will, not according to the will of the one praying. For all plans are in God's hands.

Lord, help me remember that when it comes to wills, Yours outranks and supersedes mine. For You are the One with the grand plan.

→ DATE:

Dear Heavenly Father, ...

....

....

....

....

Thank You for. . ...

....

....

....

....

....

....

....

I am worried about. . ...

....

....

....

....

....

PEOPLE I AM PRAYING FOR TODAY. . ...

....

....

....

....

....

Here's what's happening in my life. . .

I need. . .

OTHER THINGS ON MY HEART THAT
I NEED TO SHARE WITH YOU, GOD. . .

amen.
Thank You, Father,
for hearing my prayers.

Like a Child

*Whoever does not receive and accept and welcome the kingdom
of God like a little child [does] positively shall not enter it at all.*

MARK 10:15 AMPC

When people kept bringing their little ones to Jesus so that He might
touch them, the disciples tried to shoo the children away. When Jesus
saw what His twelve were doing, He was "indignant and pained"
(Mark 10:14 AMPC). This would not do. Why? Because Jesus knew
His Father's kingdom belonged to such innocents, saying, "Whoever
does not receive and accept and welcome the kingdom of God like a
little child [does] positively shall not enter it at all" (Mark 10:15 AMPC).

According to Jesus, all believers are to seek God, accept His
kingdom, and trust Him above all, just like a little one would. Followers
are to change and become like little children—humble, meek, mild,
submissive, and joyful instead of proud, overbearing, easily provoked,
obstinate, and miserable.

As you wend your way through this week's readings, think about the
ways in which you might find yourself behaving more like an adult than
a child when it comes to your prayers and praises, your faith and trust,
and your walk and talk on this side of heaven. Then consider the ways in
which you might turn back time and become the girl God created
you to be, one who sees herself as a child meek and mild—and sees
God as her Father, the One who will protect, provide for, and take
care of her today and every day.

WHO YOU REALLY ARE

What marvelous love the Father has extended to us! Just look at it—
we're called children of God! That's who we really are.

1 JOHN 3:1 MSG

You are a child of God. You were given that right because you believed in and received Jesus (John 1:12). The question is, do you see your world, life, and faith from that perspective?

Children don't worry about providing for themselves. They're not concerned about education, career objectives, car payments, mortgages, or interest payments. Kids don't regret past decisions or attempt to keep up with the Joneses. They leave the day-to-day decisions up to their caretakers who, ideally, do their best to provide for and take care of them.

Children are also quick to forgive, something most adults struggle with. Yet some adults might find it easier to forgive another person if they can view the individual who wronged them as if they were a child who must not have known any better.

Today, shift your perspective, seeing yourself and your world with the eyes of a child. Then go to prayer in that frame of mind and see what God uncovers.

Daddy God, thank You for being my Father, watching over
me, holding my hand. What shall we do today?

CHILDLIKE TRUST

"Can a mother forget the infant at her breast, walk away from the baby she bore? But even if mothers forget, I'd never forget you—never. Look, I've written your names on the backs of my hands."
ISAIAH 49:15–16 MSG

A good mother would never *not* respond to her child's cry, nor walk away from the one she so miraculously birthed into the world. Yet even if she did, God would *never* forget His child. Along with David, you can confidently say, "Even if my father and mother abandon me, the LORD cares for me" (Psalm 27:10 HCSB). Why? Because God will never forget you.

Allow those last five words to really sink into your soul: *God will never forget you.* For He is both a tender mother and a strong father to you. His love for you is constant and unchangeable because He Himself is love (1 John 4:8).

Because God is the best parent ever, you can trust Him. Just like a child. Reach for His hand when you need to be pulled up, snuggle against His chest when you need warmth, whisper your hopes and dreams when His light wakens you. Trust God like a child. He'll never forget.

I trust You, Daddy God, with my life and prayers.

CALMING YOUR SOUL

*O Lord, my heart is not proud. My eyes are not filled with
pride. And I do not trouble myself with important things or in
things too great for me. For sure I have made my soul quiet
like a child who no longer nurses while he is with his mother.
My soul within me is like a child who no longer nurses.*

PSALM 131:1–2 NLV

There are so many things in this world that humankind will never understand. So many questions that will remain unanswered. Yet you need not worry or wonder about those big questions. Your Father God has every answer. He has everything under control. So don't trouble yourself with things beyond your ken. Instead, follow Jesus' command to be as a small child, leaving all your cares, concerns, and confusion in God's hands, knowing He's in charge, knowing He has a plan not just for the world but for you and your life.

Calm the woman within you. Quiet your soul to be content with God alone, just as a child who has been weaned off her mother's milk is now calm when she lies in her mother's arms.

*Thank You, Daddy God, for handling the big questions
so I don't have to do any wondering or worrying but can
simply trust You with all my heart and rest content in You.*

69

BECOMING A CLING-ON

GOD, your God, is testing you to find out if you totally love him with everything you have in you. You are to follow only GOD, your God, hold him in deep reverence, keep his commandments, listen obediently to what he says, serve him—hold on to him for dear life!

DEUTERONOMY 13:3–4 MSG

God wants your total attention, focus, and obedience. He wants you to cling to Him as a child clings to her mother for love, affection, protection, and nourishment. You are to follow and obey God alone, serving Him, doing what He says, holding on to Him.

That's what King Hezekiah did. He "trusted in, leaned on, and was confident in the Lord. . .so that neither after him nor before him was any one of all the kings of Judah like him. For he clung and held fast to the Lord and ceased not to follow Him, but kept His commandments" (2 Kings 18:5–6 AMPC). But King Solomon, in contrast, clung to foreign women.

Some children cling to their mom, a favorite blankie, or a pacifier. But God wants you to cling to Him alone, because He is all those things—and so much more—to all His children.

I'm holding on to You, Lord, because You are my everything—in this world and the next.

CARRIED BY A GENTLE SHEPHERD

The Lord God will come with might, and His arm will rule for
Him. Behold, His reward is with Him, and His recompense
before Him. He will feed His flock like a shepherd: He will
gather the lambs in His arm, He will carry them in His
bosom and will gently lead those that have their young.

ISAIAH 40:10–11 AMPC

Imagine what life was like when you were a little baby. Your parents carried you everywhere because you couldn't walk, talk, or feed yourself. But then, as time went by, you learned to walk, talk, and do for yourself. And now here you are, a grown woman who tries to be self-sufficient, taking care of herself and others, leaving only big plans and troubles up to God. Yet for all your grown-up-ness, you're still just a little girl in God's eyes.

God wants you to look to Him alone to take care of you, carry you, help you make the big and little decisions, lead you where He'd have you go. He wants you to cling to Him with love, follow Him in word and deed, and seek Him in prayer. Today, allow your gentle Shepherd to carry you away in prayer and praise.

Here I am, Lord. Lift me in Your arms. Carry me away with You.

→ DATE:

Dear Heavenly Father, ...

....

....

....

....

Thank You for. . . ..

....

....

....

....

....

....

....

....

I am worried about. . . ..

....

....

....

....

....

PEOPLE I AM PRAYING FOR TODAY. . . ..

....

....

....

....

....

Here's what's happening in my life. . .

I need. . .

OTHER THINGS ON MY HEART THAT
I NEED TO SHARE WITH YOU, GOD. . .

Amen.
Thank You, Father,
for hearing my prayers.

God the Firewall

"'I'll be right there with her'—GOD's Decree—'a wall of fire around unwalled Jerusalem and a radiant presence within.'"
ZECHARIAH 2:5 MSG

What do you do when fear surfaces, when stress ratchets up, or when trouble enters your life? You run to God and pray to Him, in His name. Why? Because "the name of the Lord is a strong tower. The man who does what is right runs into it and is safe" (Proverbs 18:10 NLV). And because Jesus has made clear that whatever you ask in His name, He will do it (John 14:13–14).

One of the many monikers of God is found in Zechariah 2:5 (MSG), where one angel tells another that God promises to protect His people in Jerusalem, saying, "'I'll be right there with her'—GOD's Decree—'a wall of fire around unwalled Jerusalem and a radiant presence within.'"

Did you see that? God says He'll be a "wall of fire" around you for your protection. And God goes even further, promising not just to be a firewall but to be a "radiant presence within" you!

Today, meditate on Zechariah 2:5. Visualize yourself standing alone, unprotected. Then see God entering into the picture, becoming a wall of fire surrounding you from every angle, shielding you from any and every danger. Then, while you're visualizing God as your firewall, allow Him to become a warm, loving, radiant presence within you.

NIGHT-LIGHT

The LORD went ahead of them in a pillar of cloud to lead them on their way during the day and in a pillar of fire to give them light at night, so that they could travel day or night. The pillar of cloud by day and the pillar of fire by night never left its place in front of the people.
EXODUS 13:21–22 HCSB

Just as God was with the Israelites, He's with you. When you're lost, He's ready to guide you back to Him, lead you away from danger, or go ahead of you as a pillar of cloud. Then at night, God becomes the pillar of fire that chases away the shadows, keeping you safe and sound within His will and way so that you won't stub your toe, get tripped up, or lose your direction.

Today as you meditate and pray, imagine God being that pillar of fire, that night-light that not only helps you find your footing but also protects you from any shades of evil that may come your way. Remind yourself that God, the divine Creator who made all things, including you, will never leave His place in you.

Lord, You are the pillar of fire that not only protects me but shines brightly upon my way.

BURNING BUSH

The Angel of the Lord appeared to him in a flame of fire out of the midst of a bush; and he looked, and behold, the bush burned with fire, yet was not consumed. And Moses said, I will now turn aside and see this great sight, why the bush is not burned.

EXODUS 3:2–3 AMPC

. . . .

To get the attention of Moses while he was shepherding sheep in Midian, the Angel of the Lord appeared to him as a fire in a bush. The fact that the bush wasn't being consumed by the flames enticed Moses to come close and investigate the fiery bush. It was only after Moses turned off his path that "God called to him out of the midst of the bush" (Exodus 3:4 AMPC).

Sometimes God takes extreme measures to get His people's attention. For Moses, God appeared in a burning bush. That was enough to make Moses deviate from his normal path with his sheep.

Today, consider the ways God may be trying to get your attention, to speak to you, to get closer to you. Then pray for the Angel of God who blazed within the bush for Moses to reveal Himself more fully to you.

Here I am, Lord, deviating from my normal path. What would You have me see, know, learn?

A FIRE BURNING

If I say, "I won't mention Him or speak any longer in His name,"
His message becomes a fire burning in my heart, shut up in my
bones. I become tired of holding it in, and I cannot prevail. . . .
But the LORD is with me like a violent warrior. Therefore,
my persecutors will stumble and not prevail.

JEREMIAH 20:9, 11 HCSB

God chooses different ways to communicate to His people. Whenever the prophet Jeremiah would try to become mute where God was concerned, God's message within him would become like a fire burning in his heart or shut up in his bones. Tired of the pain and torture of holding in God's message, Jeremiah *had* to let God's words out—even if he got flak from his fellow humans because of it!

The encouraging part about all this is that when Jeremiah *did* speak out, God was with him. Thus, Jeremiah knew he had God's support and that no one could prevail against him.

God is still sending messages to His followers today. When you read His Word, be conscious of God's presence. When you feel His scripture burning within your heart, pay special attention. Write down His words. Then ask how He would have you get His message out.

I await Your message, Lord. Allow it to burn within my heart.

MEN ON THE ROAD TO EMMAUS

Then their eyes were opened, and they recognized Him, but
He disappeared from their sight. So they said to each other,
"Weren't our hearts ablaze within us while He was talking
with us on the road and explaining the Scriptures to us?"

LUKE 24:31–32 HCSB

After His crucifixion, Jesus appeared to a couple of His followers walking to Emmaus. For some reason, their eyes were prevented from recognizing Him. As these two individuals walked, they talked, telling their "guest" about a man named Jesus, how He had recently met His demise, and how some women now claimed His body was missing from the tomb.

That's when Jesus began explaining things to the walkers, telling them how all the scriptures had pointed to Him. When the trio came to a village, the two followers invited Jesus to stay and eat with them. It was when Jesus was blessing their food and breaking the bread that their eyes were opened. As soon as they recognized Jesus, He disappeared. That's when they realized their hearts had been burning within them as He'd explained the scriptures to them.

Today, pray for Jesus to make clear all that is unclear within His Word.

Sometimes, Lord, I have trouble understanding Your Word.
Please explain what You would have me know.

TONGUES OF FIRE

And tongues, like flames of fire that were divided, appeared to them and rested on each one of them. Then they were all filled with the Holy Spirit and began to speak in different languages, as the Spirit gave them ability for speech.

ACTS 2:3–4 HCSB

What a trying time for the disciples. Their Leader had been killed, His followers scattered. Now they were hiding in an upper room, behind locked doors, praying, perhaps wondering what was going to happen next.

Then suddenly there came the sound of a mighty wind. It filled the entire house. The next thing they knew, things described as "flames of fire" were resting on their heads. They were filled with the Holy Spirit. And they now had the ability to speak in different languages!

Dear woman, you too, if you've accepted Jesus into your heart, have been visited by the Holy Spirit. You too have God, His Son, and the Spirit living within you.

Today, ask God's Spirit to rest upon you, fill you, work within you. Ask God to make clear the abilities with which He's gifted you as you seek His will and way.

Lord, allow Your Spirit to rest upon me. Show me the gifts You would have me use as I seek Your will and way today.

→ DATE: ....

Dear Heavenly Father, ...

....

....

....

....

Thank You for. . . ..

....

....

....

....

....

....

....

I am worried about. . . ..

....

....

....

....

....

PEOPLE I AM PRAYING FOR TODAY. . . ..

....

....

....

....

....

Here's what's happening in my life. . .

....

....

....

....

I need. . .

....

....

....

....

....

....

....

....

....

....

....

....

....

....

....

OTHER THINGS ON MY HEART THAT
I NEED TO SHARE WITH YOU, GOD. . .

....

....

....

....

....

....

....

amen.
Thank You, Father,
for hearing my prayers.

Divine Dreams and Dreamers

"I will pour out My Spirit on all humanity; then your sons and your daughters will prophesy, your young men will see visions, and your old men will dream dreams. I will even pour out My Spirit on My male and female slaves in those days, and they will prophesy."

ACTS 2:17–18 HCSB

- -

God communicates with you in any number of ways, including dreams and visions! When you're sleeping, nothing can distract you from hearing what God has to say. His voice may be more easily heard, His message more understood, when it comes to you through your dreams.

On the day of Pentecost, after the fire of the Holy Spirit landed on the heads of believers in the upper room and the Spirit prompted them to speak in many different languages, onlookers thought Jesus' followers were drunk. Yet Peter made clear what God was doing by quoting the words of the prophet Joel (2:28–32). Peter was reminding the believers that God's promise to give the gift of the Holy Spirit was realized on *that* day—and continues to happen *to*day!

God is always reaching out to His people, inviting them to read His Word, believe His promises, accept and expect His help, and hear His messages through dreams, dreamers, prophets, priests, kings, preachers, servants, and others. God is looking for people with open ears, eyes, and minds.

The readings that follow will focus on divine messages received by dreamers in both the Old and New Testaments. For this week and beyond, pray before your head hits the pillow, asking God to make, through the dreams He may send your way, His desires clear.

WHO'S LISTENING?

God speaks time and again, but a person may not notice it. In a dream, a vision in the night, when deep sleep falls on people as they slumber on their beds, He uncovers their ears at that time.

JOB 33:14–16 HCSB

God is speaking to you all the time. The questions is, are you listening? Or are you too distracted by what's happening on the nonspiritual plane? It might be that your mind is too full of fretting for you to hear any words from God, including words that tell you to *stop* fretting.

Perhaps you're too busy to pay attention to Him. Wouldn't it be ironic if God were trying to get through your busyness so He could give you some tips on how to make better use of your time?

Worse than being distracted, worried, or too busy would be if you're *afraid* to hear from God. Perhaps on some level you fear He may ask you to do something you'd rather not do. Or He's just waiting to point out a bad habit you're not yet ready to break.

There could be a thousand reasons to ignore God's voice. Yet at the same time, there are ten thousand reasons to seek out His words. Choose one today.

My ears are uncovered, Lord. Please speak. Share Your wisdom.

STEPS OF FAITH

*He had a dream. He saw steps going up from the earth to heaven.
He saw the angels of God going up and down these steps. . . .
"See, I am with you." . . . Then Jacob awoke from his sleep and
said, "For sure the Lord is in this place and I did not know it."*

GENESIS 28:12, 15–16 NLV

Jacob, on the run from his brother Esau, stopped to rest at sundown. Using a stone for a pillow, Jacob fell asleep and dreamed of a stairway from earth to heaven. God's angels were going up and down it while God Himself stood above all.

In that dream, God told Jacob that He would give him and his descendants the land on which he was sleeping, that everyone on earth would be blessed through Jacob's offspring, and that God would be with him and watch over him wherever he went, promising He would not leave Jacob until He did what He'd promised him. Those are words to build your faith on.

No matter where you are or what you've done, God sees you. Because you believe in Him, He promises never to leave you until He's done what He's promised you.

Whether I'm asleep or awake, stay with me, Lord.

MIND'S AT EASE

"I dreamed a dream," Pharaoh told Joseph. "Nobody can interpret it. But I've heard that just by hearing a dream you can interpret it." Joseph answered, "Not I, but God. God will set Pharaoh's mind at ease."

GENESIS 41:15–16 MSG

You have an amazing God. He has not just perfect timing but perfect people placement. For example, Joseph had been dreaming his dreams and living with his family in Canaan when his brothers, tormented by jealousy, sold him to some traders. From there, he became a slave in the household of one of Pharaoh's officials, then landed in the dungeon based on a false allegation of rape. Through all these events, Joseph kept his head, his cool, his peace because he knew that somehow God would make everything come out okay.

And God did. Because whatever God does ends up making everything come out okay. No matter what "it" is or how long it lasts.

God has and is the ultimate wisdom. He's the One who can, will, and does set your mind at ease. He's the One who will help you understand your dreams. He's the One who will bring people into or move them out of your life at just the right time.

You, Lord, are the truth and wisdom I seek. Ease my mind, I pray.

ANOTHER ROUTE

When they saw the star, they rejoiced exceedingly with great joy. And going into the house, they saw the child with Mary his mother, and they fell down and worshiped him. . . . Being warned in a dream not to return to Herod, they departed to their own country by another way.
MATTHEW 2:10–12 ESV

Wise men from the east had followed a star to Jerusalem, looking to worship the One who'd been born king of the Jews. When King Herod heard of this other "king," he became very jealous. So he asked the wise men to continue their search and let him know when they found this child king. Although Herod said he wanted to worship the new "king," what he really wanted to do was kill off his competition.

On their way once more, the wise men continued to follow the star and found the Child Jesus. Thrilled, they worshipped Him and gave Him their gifts of gold, frankincense, and myrrh. Then, through a dream, God warned the wise men not to go back to Herod. So they went home by another route.

When you're praying for direction, keep your eyes and ears open, heeding God's warnings in whatever form they take.

Open my eyes and ears to the route You'd have me take, Lord.

FOUR TIMES

An angel of the Lord appeared to him in a dream, saying, "Joseph, son of David, do not fear to take Mary as your wife." . . . An angel of the Lord appeared to Joseph in a dream and said, "Rise, take the child and his mother, and flee to Egypt." . . . An angel of the Lord appeared in a dream to Joseph in Egypt, saying, "Rise, take the child and his mother and go to the land of Israel.". . . Being warned in a dream he withdrew to the district of Galilee.

MATTHEW 1:20; 2:13, 19–20, 22 ESV

Four different times an angel of God appeared to Joseph in a dream and directed this stepfather in how to protect the Son of God.

The first occasion came when Joseph was considering not marrying an already pregnant Mary. God came and explained the situation, and Joseph followed His directions. After Jesus' birth, the angel of God came to Joseph three more times, telling him where to flee and not to be afraid.

Need direction? Keep your mind open to God and His voice, even when you sleep.

Speak to me in whatever way You will, Lord.
Show me what You would have me do, where You
would have me go. In Jesus' name, amen.

→ DATE:

Dear Heavenly Father, ...

....

....

....

....

Thank You for. . ...

....

....

....

....

....

....

....

....

I am worried about. . ...

....

....

....

....

....

PEOPLE I AM PRAYING FOR TODAY. . ...

....

....

....

....

....

Here's what's happening in my life. . ...
....
....
....
....

I need. . ...

....

....

....

....

OTHER THINGS ON MY HEART THAT
I NEED TO SHARE WITH YOU, GOD. . .

....

....

....

....

....

....

....

....

....

....

....

amen.
Thank You, Father,
for hearing my prayers.

God the Sure Foundation

Therefore the Lord GOD said: "Look, I have laid a stone in Zion, a tested stone, a precious cornerstone, a sure foundation; the one who believes will be unshakable."
ISAIAH 28:16 HCSB

Some days it takes a strong stomach to look at the headlines, turn on the TV, switch on the radio, or check the latest reports on your favorite news website. There seems to be no good news—at all!

That phrase—*no good news*—may sound right to some people but not to those who have faith in the Father, Son, and Holy Spirit. For those believers know and live a life of hope because their God is the everlasting, uncompromising, perfect, steady Rock.

No matter what craziness is taking place in this world, God has promised a firm and fixed place, a sturdy Rock upon which you can stand. There you can live and love during times of uncertainty and instability. There you will be safe and cared for, protected and adored.

When you feel like you're all alone, in too deep, beginning to sink, cry out to God. Ask Him to pull you up and set you down upon that precious cornerstone He's laid for you. Then you'll find your footing once again upon the eternal, sure, and unshakable foundation that is Christ.

MOUNTAINTOP REFUGE

*God is bedrock under my feet, the castle in which I live, my
rescuing knight. My God—the high crag where I run for dear
life, hiding behind the boulders, safe in the granite hideout;
my mountaintop refuge, he saves me from ruthless men. I sing
to God the Praise-Lofty, and find myself safe and saved.*

2 Samuel 22:2–4 MSG

When you feel as if your reality is slipping away, that you can no
longer get a foothold in this journey called life, that stress has seemingly overtaken you, stop. In your tracks. And find your way to God
quickly. Get to Him before you lose your footing.

Call out to God. Listen for His reply. Envision Him as the castle,
the fortress built on the solid rock upon which you live, move, and
have your being. See your God as the knight you've been waiting
for all your life! And run into His arms. There in your mountaintop
refuge, no one can reach you, find you, harm you. There you are
safe. . .and home.

*Creator of heaven and earth, You are my place of safety, my
solid rock, my home, my castle, my knight in shining armor. It's to
You I run, for You I live, in You I trust and pray in Jesus' name.*

STEADIED

I waited patiently and expectantly for the Lord; and He inclined to me and heard my cry. He drew me up out of a horrible pit [a pit of tumult and of destruction], out of the miry clay (froth and slime), and set my feet upon a rock, steadying my steps and establishing my goings.

PSALM 40:1–2 AMPC

God doesn't want you to trust Him just some of the time. He wants you trusting Him *all* of the time. That calls for patience and faith on your part—and lots of it. For if you don't have patience and aren't trusting that God will work things out for good for you in His time, chances are you'll try to take things into your own hands and do them your own way, or the way you think God would do them. The next thing you know, you may be walking out of His will and way.

Stop the madness before it starts by growing both your patience and your faith. As you wait expectantly, know God has heard your prayer. That He will draw you out of your tough spot and set you upon Christ. He'll put your feet on the Rock who steadies your steps, both coming and going.

In You, Lord, I can be Rock steady.
In You I trust and wait.

ROCK OF REFUGE

In You, O Lord, do I put my trust and seek refuge; let me never be put to shame or [have my hope in You] disappointed; deliver me in Your righteousness! Bow down Your ear to me, deliver me speedily! Be my Rock of refuge, a strong Fortress to save me!

PSALM 31:1–2 AMPC

Imagine you're having a really bad day. Nothing seems to be going right. And at the end of it, you're more than discouraged. You're feeling lost, untethered. You're filled with apprehension, afraid to take another step forward because you feel as if you're already walking on shaky ground. When your day is going more wrong than right, take a dip into the Psalms. Find one that speaks so much to your heart and soul that you yourself could've written it!

Today, see God as your "granite cave," your "hiding place," your "high cliff nest," your "place of safety" (Psalm 31:2 MSG). As you pray, imagine God bending down, His ear close to your mouth. Be sure He's heard everything you've said—as well as everything you *haven't* said. Believe God knows exactly what to do and when to do it. Then stand tall and steady on your Rock of Refuge.

Lord, be my Rock of Refuge, my place of safety, my strength and deliverer. Amen.

THE SPIRITUAL ROCK

*Our fathers were all under the cloud, and all passed
through the sea, and all were baptized into Moses in the
cloud and in the sea, and all ate the same spiritual food, and
all drank the same spiritual drink. For they drank from the
spiritual Rock that followed them, and the Rock was Christ.*

1 CORINTHIANS 10:1–4 ESV

When the people of Israel left Egypt, the cloud that led them away
from slavery was God. It was also He who worked through Moses to
part the sea so that the Israelites could escape. Once they reached
the other side of the Red Sea, God was in the cloud that continued
to lead them by day and in the fire that led them at night.

As God's people then wandered through the wilderness, God
continued to trek with them, leading them, protecting them, providing
spiritual food and drink for them. And that spiritual drink was Christ,
ever present, supplying the people's need for water from the very
beginning of their journey (Exodus 17:1–7) and when they neared
the end (Numbers 20:2–13).

Just as God and Jesus led, protected, provided for, and delivered
the Israelites, They lead, protect, provide for, and deliver you. Every
moment of every day. From beginning to end.

*Lead me, God. Protect and defend me. Jesus, quench my thirst.
Be my spiritual Rock and my everlasting fountain. Amen.*

FOUNDATIONAL BELIEFS

*"These words I speak to you are not incidental additions
to your life, homeowner improvements to your standard
of living. They are foundational words, words to build a
life on. If you work these words into your life, you are like
a smart carpenter who built his house on solid rock."*

MATTHEW 7:24 MSG

. . . .

If you're standing on shaky ground, you may want to inspect your
foundation. What are you building your life on?

Jesus told His followers that if they build their lives on His words,
they will be wise, prudent, and smart like a carpenter who builds
his house on a *solid* rock. Then when the rain poured and the river
flooded and the winds pounded the house, it didn't collapse. Because
its foundation was on a solid rock. A rock that wouldn't move no
matter what came up against it.

Yet if followers don't build their lives on His words, if they don't
work them into the fabric of their very lives, they will be like the
stupid carpenter who built his house on the sand. When the rains
came and the waters rose, the house collapsed.

Today, consider your life. Are you on the solid rock or the sand?

*Open my eyes, Lord, to what I've built my life on.
Help me shore up my faith in and on You. Amen.*

→ DATE:

Dear Heavenly Father, ...

....

....

....

....

Thank You for. . . ..

....

....

....

....

....

....

....

....

I am worried about. . . ..

....

....

....

....

....

....

PEOPLE I AM PRAYING FOR TODAY. . . ..

....

....

....

....

....

Here's what's happening in my life. . .

I need. . .

OTHER THINGS ON MY HEART THAT
I NEED TO SHARE WITH YOU, GOD. . .

amen.
Thank You, Father,
for hearing my prayers.

Beyond All We Ask, Hope, or Imagine

*God can do anything, you know—far more than you could
ever imagine or guess or request in your wildest dreams!*
EPHESIANS 3:20 MSG

God has so much power. And it's that power, His power, working within you and all other believers, that carries out His purpose and does "superabundantly, far over and above all that we [dare] ask or think [infinitely beyond our highest prayers, desires, thoughts, hopes, or dreams]" (Ephesians 3:20 AMPC).

Just pause a moment. Think about God's power working within you, doing things beyond anything you'd ever ask for, hope for, or imagine. . . .

God proves His power on every page of the Bible. God instills His power within His people every moment of their lives, if only believers would expect, receive, allow that power. If only they would give God free rein to do what He will in, with, and through them. Putting no limits on Him, forcing no particular situation in order to derive a certain outcome.

God wants you (and the rest of His believers) to *believe* He can do anything; to *acknowledge* He has the best answer to your particular situation; and to *expect* the unexpected hand of God to move in your life. In Jesus' name.

GREAT AND MIGHTY THINGS

Thus says the Lord Who made [the earth], the Lord Who formed it to establish it—the Lord is His name: Call to Me and I will answer you and show you great and mighty things, fenced in and hidden, which you do not know (do not distinguish and recognize, have knowledge of and understand).

JEREMIAH 33:2–3 AMPC

- -

Whatever you need, whatever information, wisdom, knowledge, ideas, help, plans, answers you require, God is here for you. God is waiting to hear your voice call out His name. Tired of standing on the sidelines, God is waiting for you to call Him into the game, to allow Him to play a leading role in your story.

When you *do* call on God, inviting Him into your life with its victories and quandaries, He will respond by loving you, calming you, enlightening you, and opening your eyes to things you may have missed—strange, mighty, and mysterious things that leave you breathless.

Today, pray to your amazing Creator. Call on His name. Know that He who formed the earth will answer you in His time.

Creator of all, as I come before You, show me great and mighty things.

NO DAY LIKE IT

The sun stopped in the center of the sky. It did not hurry to go down for about a whole day. There has been no day like it before or since, when the Lord listened to the voice of a man. For the Lord fought for Israel.

JOSHUA 10:13–14 NLV

As Joshua and the Israelites began making their way into the Promised Land, five kings came to Gibeon to battle them. So God reassured Joshua, telling him, "Do not be afraid of them. For I have given them into your hands" (Joshua 10:8 NLV).

Then, for His part, God threw the enemies of His people into a panic, raining down large hailstones when the soldiers tried to flee. As it turned out, "more died from the hail-stones than the sons of Israel killed with the sword" (Joshua 10:11 NLV)!

Yet then, in the midst of the battle, "Joshua spoke to the Lord. . .He said, in the eyes of Israel, 'O sun, stand still at Gibeon. O moon, stand still in the valley of Aijalon'" (Joshua 10:12 NLV). And God answered Joshua's prayer, making the sun stand still until His people's enemies were defeated.

Just as God fought for Joshua then, He fights for you now.

With You battling beside me, Lord, I'm not afraid.

INVISIBLE PROTECTORS

[Elisha] answered, Fear not; for those with us are more than those with them. Then Elisha prayed, Lord, I pray You, open his eyes that he may see. And the Lord opened the young man's eyes, and he saw, and behold, the mountain was full of horses and chariots of fire round about Elisha.

2 KINGS 6:16–17 AMPC

At times, you may have difficulty perceiving what God may be preparing to do. And there you are, in a tough situation where there appears to be no way out. Before allowing panic to set in, consider making an Elisha move.

As the story goes, Elisha kept thwarting the king of Syria's military moves against Israel. For that prophet kept giving the Syrian army's position away to the king of Israel. Hearing that Elisha was in Dothan, the Syrian king sent his horses, chariots, charioteers, and army to the city. And one night they surrounded it.

When Elisha's servant saw the army, horses, and chariots, he panicked, asking Elisha what they should do. That's when the prophet prayed and God answered, allowing the servant to see God's invisible protectors all around them.

Live knowing God is always on the move. Pray knowing He can do anything. Rest easy knowing His invisible protectors surround you.

Open my eyes, Lord, so that I may see.

TEN STEPS BACK

Isaiah said, "This is the sign to you from the LORD that He will do what He has promised: Should the shadow go ahead 10 steps or go back 10 steps?"

2 KINGS 20:9 HCSB

. . . .

The prophet Isaiah, speaking for God, told Judah's ailing King Hezekiah, "Set your house in order because you'll soon be dead." Hearing those words, the king turned his face toward the wall and prayed, "Please LORD, remember how I have walked before You faithfully and wholeheartedly and have done what pleases You" (2 Kings 20:3 HCSB). Then he began crying bitter tears.

Before Isaiah had even left the inner courtyard, God told him, "Go back and tell Hezekiah. . .'I have heard your prayer; I have seen your tears. Look, I will heal you. . . . I will add 15 years to your life'" (20:5–6 HCSB). When Hezekiah asked the prophet for a sign that God would do as promised, Isaiah "called out to the LORD, and He brought the shadow back the 10 steps it had descended" (20:11 HCSB).

God hears your prayers. He sees your tears. He will come through on His promises, no matter how impossible their fulfillment appears.

Thank You, Lord, for hearing my prayers, seeing my tears, and doing the seemingly impossible.

GREAT EXPECTATIONS

*Peter directed his gaze intently at him, and so did John, and said,
Look at us! And [the man] paid attention to them, expecting that
he was going to get something from them. But Peter said, Silver and
gold (money) I do not have; but what I do have, that I give to you.*
ACTS 3:4–6 AMPC

One afternoon, disciples Peter and John headed to the temple for prayer. It was there, at the Beautiful gate, that they saw a man who'd been crippled from birth. Lying there, he begged for alms from people entering the temple.

When the man saw Peter and John about to enter the temple, he asked them for money. Peter and John both stared at him. Then Peter said, "Look at us!" So the lame man did look at the disciples, fully expecting to receive something from them. But what he got was not expected—at all! For Peter told him he had no money. But what he did have he was more than happy to give the man. And that was Peter's invoking the name of Jesus Christ so the man would be healed—and he was!

When you pray, expect the unexpected from Jesus. Have great expectations!

*You know what I need better than I do, Lord.
Thus, to You I pray, expecting the unexpected!*

→ DATE:

Dear Heavenly Father, ...

....

....

....

....

Thank You for. . . ..

....

....

....

....

....

....

....

....

I am worried about. . . ..

....

....

....

....

....

....

PEOPLE I AM PRAYING FOR TODAY. . . ..

....

....

....

....

....

Here's what's happening in my life. . .

I need. . .

OTHER THINGS ON MY HEART THAT
I NEED TO SHARE WITH YOU, GOD. . .

Amen.
Thank You, Father,
for hearing my prayers.

WEEK 13

Calm Waters

They cried to the LORD in their trouble, and he delivered them from their distress. He made the storm be still, and the waves of the sea were hushed. Then they were glad that the waters were quiet, and he brought them to their desired haven.

PSALM 107:28–30 ESV

In Psalm 107:23–32, the writer talks about how God's people went to the sea in ships to conduct trade with other countries. Yet the sailors were caught in a storm. But they cried out to God and He heard their prayer. He hushed the storm, and the sea waters, calmed under His hand and word, became still. People aboard the ship gave thanks that the waters had grown quiet. Then God brought them to the harbor they'd been longing for.

The words of Psalm 107 were written over three thousand years ago. And it was over two thousand years ago that Jesus' followers found themselves out in a storm while on the waters and cried out to God for deliverance. Jesus delivered these sailors by calming the wind and the waves and then brought them to the place they'd been striving for.

You, like Jesus' followers, might sometimes find yourself in an untenable situation, one in which your only recourse is to cry out to God, trying to get Him to hear you over the havoc and chaos happening all around you. But take heart. Jesus is with you, hears you, and will respond. Simply have faith.

106

THE MAN WITH THE PLAN

When the people saw the sign (miracle) that Jesus had performed, they began saying, Surely and beyond a doubt this is the Prophet Who is to come into the world! Then Jesus, knowing that they meant to come and seize Him that they might make Him king, withdrew again to the hillside by Himself alone.

JOHN 6:14–15 AMPC

Before being caught up in a powerful storm, the disciples had been hanging with Jesus on a mountainside. When a huge crowd of people arrived on the scene, Jesus had them sit on the grass. He then took a boy's loaves and fishes, blessed them, and was able to feed five thousand men plus women and children! Even more amazing is that twelve baskets of leftovers were gathered!

That's when the people determined Jesus was the predicted prophet (Deuteronomy 18:15, 18). But Jesus, not wanting to become involved in a violent uprising against the Romans, went off by Himself into the hills.

God knows His sons and daughters have limited knowledge, that they may make erroneous assumptions while on their faith walk. Fortunately, Jesus, the Man with the plan, can set them straight. All they have to do is ask.

Lord, when I pray, please set me straight. Align my thoughts and plans with Yours. In Jesus' name, amen.

ALREADY ON HIS WAY

When evening came, His disciples went down to the sea, and they took a boat and were going across the sea to Capernaum. It was now dark, and still Jesus had not [yet] come back to them.

JOHN 6:16–17 AMPC

The story of Jesus as a water-walker is covered in Matthew 14:22–33; Mark 6:45–52; *and* John 6:16–21. When Matthew tells it, he writes that Jesus had "directed the disciples to get into the boat and go before Him to the other side, while He sent away the crowds" (14:22 AMPC)—and Mark's account backs up Matthew's (6:45). But Mark's goes even further in detail, telling readers that while Jesus was still on land, He'd seen His disciples "were troubled and tormented in [their] rowing, for the wind was against them"; and because they were in trouble, Jesus "came to them, walking [directly] on the sea" (Mark 6:48 AMPC).

This story is a reminder that even before you cry out to Jesus, He sees you. He knows what's happening in your life, the troubles you face, the challenges surrounding you. And because of this, your loving Jesus is already making plans to rescue you. He's already headed your way.

Thank You, Lord, for seeing me, loving me, saving me.
For already being on Your way to have, to help, to hold. Amen.

CLOSER THAN YOU THINK

*The sea was getting rough and rising high because of a great
and violent wind that was blowing. [However] when they had
rowed three or four miles, they saw Jesus walking on the sea and
approaching the boat. And they were afraid (terrified). But Jesus
said to them, It is I; be not afraid! [I AM; stop being frightened!]*

JOHN 6:18–20 AMPC

How many times have you been at least halfway through a difficult challenge when a storm or some other kind of trouble threatened not just to waylay you but to overcome you? That's where Jesus' closest followers found themselves.

Jesus had sent His followers out to the boat, telling them to head for the other shore. Now they were having trouble not just rowing against the wind but merely staying afloat! And some of these disciples were seasoned fishermen! Yet here they were, in dire trouble.

Then the men see what seems like a ghost, an apparition! They cry out in fear, shrieking even louder when the strange being approaches their craft. But then they hear Jesus' voice and words: "It is I, the I AM; stop being so afraid!"

No matter how deep you feel you're sinking, seek out Jesus. He's closer than you think.

*I'm seeking You out, Jesus, listening for
Your voice. Please speak. Amen.*

EASE OF PASSAGE

Then they were quite willing and glad for Him to come into the boat. And now the boat went at once to the land they had steered toward. [And immediately they reached the shore toward which they had been slowly making their way.]

JOHN 6:21 AMPC

In the beginning of the disciples' journey across the waters, Jesus was still on shore. In fact, as His followers had launched out to sea, Jesus had headed in the opposite direction: up the hilltop. He did so not only to escape the crowds who wanted to crown Him king but to get some alone time with Father God.

Unfortunately for the disciples, their seafaring journey wasn't going as smoothly as they'd hoped. The winds and waves had picked up power, and they and their watercraft were being pushed around violently.

Yet once Jesus appeared on the scene and they allowed Him to come onto their boat, the journey went much smoother. So easy was their passage, so calm the water, that "immediately they reached the shore toward which they had been slowly making their way."

Make it a point every day to recognize, to remember, to invite, to pray Jesus into your boat. Before you know it, you'll be where you were meant to be.

Be with me, Lord, upon the waters. In You I find an easier and calmer passage.

WATER WALKING 101

Peter got out of the boat and walked on the water, and he came toward Jesus. But when he perceived and felt the strong wind, he was frightened, and. . .he began to sink.

MATTHEW 14:29–30 AMPC

Matthew 14:22–33; Mark 6:45–52; and John 6:16–21 contain the story of Jesus walking on the water. But only one includes Peter doing some water walking on his own.

It started when Jesus sent the disciples ahead of Him, out to sea, while He went up a hill to pray alone. When He saw the boys were having trouble, Jesus walked out on the water to reach them. They screamed, thinking He was a ghost. But Jesus said, "Take courage! I Am! Stop being afraid!" (Matthew 14:27 AMPC).

While the storm raged, Peter said, "Lord, if it is You, command me to come to You on the water" (14:28 AMPC). So Jesus said, "Come!" and soon Peter himself was water walking. But as soon as he turned his eyes from Jesus to the wind and waves, he began to sink, crying out, "Lord, save me!" "Instantly Jesus reached out His hand and caught and held him" (14:31 AMPC).

Thus, rule number one in water walking: Keep your eyes on Jesus.

My faith and eyes are focused on You, Jesus. Let's walk.

→ DATE:

Dear Heavenly Father, ...
....
....
....
....

Thank You for. . . ..
....
....
....
....
....
....
....
....

I am worried about. . . ..
....
....
....
....
....

PEOPLE I AM PRAYING FOR TODAY. . . ..
....
....
....
....
....

Here's what's happening in my life. . .

I need. . .

OTHER THINGS ON MY HEART THAT
I NEED TO SHARE WITH YOU, GOD. . .

amen.
Thank You, Father,
for hearing my prayers.

The Word Trust

The Lord gave them peace on every side, just as He had promised their fathers. . . . Every good promise which the Lord had made to the people of Israel came true.

JOSHUA 21:44–45 NLV

The God you serve, the God you love, the God to whom you pray keeps His promises—what He says He will do, He will actually do. No matter how strange or seemingly impossible one of God's promises may sound, you can believe it.

Because God is always true to His Word, you can *trust* Him to do what He has said He will do. God had told His people, the Israelites, that He would make them a great people, beyond counting. That He would bring them to a land flowing with milk and honey, a land in which they would be a free people. His people.

All the promises God had made regarding the Promised Land, He brought to fruition. The Israelites now had their own territories where they could settle with their families and serve God. He "gave them peace on every side, just as He had promised their fathers. . . . Every good promise which the Lord had made to the people of Israel came true" (Joshua 21:44–45 NLV).

If you too want peace on every side, trust God to be true to His Word—to come through on the promises He has made to you, as well as to those you love.

GRANTOR OF GOOD

*Blessed be the Lord, Who has given rest to His people Israel,
according to all that He promised. Not one word has failed
of all His good promise which He promised through Moses
His servant. May the Lord our God be with us as He was
with our fathers; may He not leave us or forsake us.*

1 KINGS 8:56–57 AMPC

Today's verses are words King Solomon spoke to God and His people the day the temple was dedicated. Solomon recognized God—not his father, David, nor any other man—was the One who had given rest and peace to His people. It was He who gave the people hope, courage, protection, and guidance as they traveled through the wilderness and finally made their way into the Promised Land. And He did that by speaking to them, making them promises, and coming through on those promises.

Then Solomon prayed that this God who had led His people to this place, this grantor of good promises, would never leave them.

Today, consider which of God's good promises means the most to you. Then write a prayer around that promise. Here's a prayer based around Isaiah 43:2's promise:

*Lord, be with me as I go through the flood and
fire. Bring me out whole on the other side.*

GOD SPEAKS

*I am the Lord; I will speak, and the word that I shall speak
shall be performed (come to pass); it shall be no more delayed
or prolonged, for in your days, O rebellious house, I will
speak the word and will perform it, says the Lord God.*

EZEKIEL 12:25 AMPC

God speaks, and chaos becomes order. God speaks, saying, "Let there be light," and there is light. God, the One who "makes the dead live again. . .speaks, and something is made out of nothing" (Romans 4:17 NLV). That's God's might. That's His power, the power you can tap into through prayer.

Whatever God speaks, whatever promise emits from His mouth, He makes it come to pass. The Lord speaks, and His words become reality.

Through prayer, you can speak creative words into your own life. And the most power-filled words you can speak and pray are those found in God's Word. If you're fearful about not having enough, pray, "The LORD is my shepherd; there is nothing I lack" (Psalm 23:1 HCSB). If you need courage, pray, "The LORD is on my side; I will not fear. What can man do to me?" (Psalm 118:6 ESV). Speak God's Word into your life, and He will ensure your prayer according to His Word becomes reality!

*"You will keep the mind that is dependent on You in
perfect peace, for it is trusting in You" (Isaiah 26:3 HCSB).*

PROSPER IN PURPOSE

As the rain and snow. . .make [the earth] bring forth and
sprout, that it may give seed to the sower and bread to the
eater, so shall My word be that goes forth out of My mouth:
it shall not return to Me void [without producing any effect,
useless], but it shall accomplish that which I please and
purpose, and it shall prosper in the thing for which I sent it.

ISAIAH 55:10–11 AMPC

God's Word is alive, cutting things down and building things up. So it only makes sense that when God's Word goes forth out of His mouth, something happens. Things are put into motion. Because the things God says accomplish exactly what He wants them to accomplish.

The words you say, the words you think, have an effect as well. The words you say can bring life (Proverbs 15:4), soothe the soul and body (Proverbs 16:24), and refresh other people (Proverbs 18:4)—or do the exact opposite.

When you pray, believe in the power of God's words—and make your prayer one that will please Him and prosper in His purpose.

Thank You, Lord, for giving strength and
power to the weak and weary (Isaiah 40:29).

MISSION POSSIBLE

"Your cousin Elizabeth conceived a son. . . . Everyone called her barren, and here she is six months pregnant! Nothing, you see, is impossible with God." And Mary said, "Yes, I see it all now: I'm the Lord's maid, ready to serve. Let it be with me just as you say." Then the angel left her.

LUKE 1:36–38 MSG

How wonderful to know that nothing is ever impossible when God is on the scene. And He is here—and there! He, God, the Creator of the universe, is everywhere. Even within you. God is above, under, beside, in, and around you at this very moment. And with Him in your life, nothing will ever be impossible: "No word from God shall be without power or impossible of fulfillment" (Luke 1:37 AMPC). Because of God, chaos is controlled, peace is found in the midst of mayhem (think eye of a hurricane), and the least is the greatest. With God, anything is possible.

Make up your mind about that. Remember, each and every day, as soon as your feet hit the floor, that with God in your life, nothing is impossible.

With You, Lord, my life, my mission, my dream is possible! I, Your servant, am ready! Let things be as You say!

WORD UP!

All people are like grass. Their greatness is like the flowers. The grass dries up and the flowers fall off. But the Word of the Lord will last forever. That Word is the Good News which was preached to you.

1 PETER 1:24–25 NLV

It's alarming, really, how quickly people move in and out of our lives. These days people are much more mobile, much more willing to move out of and then into a new location, job, or relationship. No matter how much we say we don't like change, we are on the cusp of change, if not actually going through change, each and every day of our lives. Seeing how much and how quickly our lives and the world around us change can feel a bit disconcerting.

Thank God there is one thing—actually, technically two things—that never change: God and His Word.

People—known and unknown—come and go. They are here one day and gone the next. Any fame or fortune is left behind. For people, like grass, eventually die. They disappear from our lives if not our hearts and minds. But God and His Word will always be there to boost us up, heal our hearts, and soothe our souls and spirits. He will never let us down.

Boost me, Lord. Fill me with Your Good News! Amen!

Dear Heavenly Father, ...

....

....

....

....

Thank You for. . . ..

....

....

....

....

....

....

....

I am worried about. . . ..

....

....

....

....

....

PEOPLE I AM PRAYING FOR TODAY. . . ..

....

....

....

....

Here's what's happening in my life. . ...
....
....
....
....

I need. . ...
....
....
....
....
....
....
....
....
....
....
....
....
....
....
....
....
....
....

OTHER THINGS ON MY HEART THAT
I NEED TO SHARE WITH YOU, GOD. . .

....
....
....
....
....
....
....
....

Amen.
Thank You, Father,
for hearing my prayers.

Ladies in Waiting

For it is not yet time for it to come true. The time is coming in a hurry, and it will come true. If you think it is slow in coming, wait for it. For it will happen for sure, and it will not wait.

HABAKKUK 2:3 NLV

Waiting. It can be hard to do, especially today when, with the click of a button, our desires can be ordered, fulfilled, and received within twenty-four hours. And all without needing to leave our home or speak to another human being.

In the Bible, we read story after story about women desiring yet waiting decades to secure a husband, bear a child, and find healing. Others spent years dreaming and eagerly awaiting a heavenly Deliverer. Some women waited patiently. Others, who had trust issues, took matters into their own hands. Some worked on a quid-pro-quo basis: "Lord, You give me this, and I'll give You that." Interestingly enough, all of them prayed for God's help, eager to gain His ear and plead with Him to remember them and their plight.

This week we'll look at five women, four of whom are waiting on God to open up their wombs. Only the last, an elderly widow, is waiting not for a child of her own but for One who would redeem Israel.

Regardless of what you're waiting for or how long you've been waiting, never give up the cause. Just keep your hope in and your focus on God and what He can do and have faith. Give God time to move. Be prepared, if necessary, to be God's lady in waiting.

GOD RESTORES SARAH

God said to Abraham, "Why did Sarah laugh saying, 'Me?
Have a baby? An old woman like me?' Is anything too hard for God?
I'll be back about this time next year and Sarah will have a baby."
GENESIS 18:13–14 MSG

The beautiful Sarah had hitched her wagon to Abraham's star. And it was to him that God promised blessings and children beyond number (Genesis 15:1–6). Yet both Abraham and Sarah continued growing old, the years quickly ticking by. Still Sarah remained childless.

Finally, Sarah took matters into her own hands. She gave her servant Hagar to Abraham, telling him, "Now see, the Lord has kept me from having children. Go in to the woman who serves me. It may be that I will get children through her" (Genesis 16:2 NLV). Abraham took her advice and Hagar became pregnant. . .and a bit belligerent at the same time, as she began to look down on her own mistress. This prompted Sarah to begin mistreating Hagar. In response, Hagar ran away, only to encounter God, who told her to go back.

Sarah did eventually bear a son, Isaac, by Abraham. She'd finally acquired more faith in God's plans than in her own.

Help me be still as I patiently and faithfully wait on You, Lord.

123

GOD REMEMBERS RACHEL

Then God remembered Rachel and answered her
pleading and made it possible for her to have children. . . .
She became pregnant and bore a son; and she said, God has
taken away my reproach, disgrace, and humiliation.

GENESIS 30:22–23 AMPC

. . . .

For years Rachel competed with her sister, Leah, in bearing children to Jacob. When Rachel remained barren, she said to Jacob, "Here is my slave Bilhah. Go sleep with her, and she'll bear children for me so that through her I too can build a family" (Genesis 30:3 HCSB). Jacob agreed and Bilhah conceived, eventually delivering a son named Dan. When Bilhah bore a second son to Jacob, Rachel said, "With mighty wrestlings [in prayer to God] I have struggled with my sister and have prevailed" (Genesis 30:8 AMPC).

Yet after Bilhah's two sons, five more children were born to Jacob by Zilpah (Leah's servant) and by Leah before God remembered Rachel, making her able to bear Joseph and later Benjamin (Genesis 35:16–19).

Whenever the Bible says "God remembered," it's a signal that He is about to do something to benefit that person. It means that person has reached a turning point in her life. No matter how long something takes or how impossible a solution sounds, don't give up. Keep praying. Trust that God will remember you.

Lord, hear my prayer. . .again.

GOD RESPONDS TO HANNAH

Hannah became pregnant and in due time bore a
son and named him Samuel [heard of God].

1 SAMUEL 1:20 AMPC

Elkanah had two wives: Hannah and Peninnah. Hannah was childless. Peninnah had children. Yet Elkanah loved Hannah the most.

Every year Elkanah would take his family with him to Shiloh to worship God. And every year Peninnah would bully the barren Hannah to the point of tears.

Then one year at Shiloh, Hannah "was deeply distressed and prayed to the LORD and wept bitterly" (1 Samuel 1:10 ESV). She asked God to remember her and give her a son, promising that if He did so, she would give that same son right back to God. After she'd poured out her soul to God, Eli the priest blessed her request, saying, "Go in peace, and the God of Israel grant your petition that you have made to him" (1 Samuel 1:17 ESV). And God did!

Hannah conceived, bore, and weaned Samuel, gave him over to God, and then prayed and sang a song of joy and victory! Because she asked, she received. . .eventually. So will you—if you ask God with the right motives.

Help me be both wise and patient, Lord, as I pray to You.

125

GOD REJUVENATES ELIZABETH

The angel said to him, "Zacharias, do not be afraid.
Your prayer has been heard. Your wife Elizabeth will
give birth to a son. You are to name him John."

LUKE 1:13 NLV

Although childless and well up in years, Zacharias and Elizabeth were believers leading a righteous and blameless life in God.

Then one day Zachariah was fulfilling his priestly duties in the temple, and the angel Gabriel appeared. He announced that Zacharias and his wife would soon conceive a child. Only thing was, Zacharias didn't believe him. So Gabriel muted Zacharias until the day John was born.

Later, Mary visited Elizabeth. And "when Elizabeth heard Mary speak, the baby moved in her body. At the same time Elizabeth was filled with the Holy Spirit" (Luke 1:41 NLV). Imagine being well up in years and six months pregnant. And the baby within you leaps with joy when your cousin Mary comes to call!

God makes plans and provides for His people as He works out His will and way. And He does so regardless of all those things we might consider obstacles. Never give up hope that God can and will revitalize your situation someday.

Hear my prayer, Lord. Rejuvenate me and my
situation as I wait with hope in You. Amen.

GOD REWARDS ANNA

*Anna the prophetess was also there, a daughter of Phanuel from
the tribe of Asher. She was by now a very old woman. She had been
married seven years and a widow for eighty-four. She never left the
Temple area, worshiping night and day with her fastings and prayers.*
LUKE 2:36–37 MSG

Imagine being a very old widow who has spent eighty-four years
worshipping day and night at the temple, doing nothing but fasting
and praying. The prophetess Anna is on the scene when Joseph and
Mary bring little Jesus into the temple. They are there, in accordance
with God's law, to present Jesus to God and to offer a sacrifice. That's
when Simeon, another devout individual, sees Jesus, takes Him into
his arms, and begins praying to and blessing God. For Simeon had
also been waiting to see the Lord's Christ.

After seeing Jesus and recognizing Him as the Christ, Anna,
at that very moment, begins to thank God and to spread the word
that the One they'd been waiting for had finally arrived (Luke 2:38).

God rewards those who seek Him out (Hebrews 11:6). What
might you be waiting for or seeking?

*As I continue on in my faith walk, Lord, give me patience.
Help me never lose hope in You and Your reward, Lord.*

→ DATE:

Dear Heavenly Father,

....

....

....

....

Thank You for. . .

....

....

....

....

....

....

....

....

I am worried about. . .

....

....

....

....

....

....

PEOPLE I AM PRAYING FOR TODAY. . .

....

....

....

....

....

....

Here's what's happening in my life. . .

....

....

....

....

I need. ....

....

....

....

....

....

....

....

....

....

....

....

....

....

....

....

....

....

OTHER THINGS ON MY HEART THAT
I NEED TO SHARE WITH YOU, GOD. . .

....

....

....

....

....

....

....

....

Amen.
Thank You, Father,
for hearing my prayers.

Meanwhile, Pray

And it shall be that before they call I will answer;
and while they are yet speaking I will hear.
ISAIAH 65:24 AMPC

In Isaiah 65:24 (AMPC), the Lord said through the prophet Isaiah, "And it shall be that before they call I will answer; and while they are yet speaking I will hear." Imagine that. Before you even approach God with any kind of a prayer request, He has already answered. While you're still trying to get the words (or moans and groans) out of your mouth, God has already heard them.

Prayer, the unique form of communication between you and your Creator, is that powerful. Before you have even begun to think about what you want to ask God or the secrets you want to confess, He knows what's in your mind and what's going to come out. And He's already been taking action, working in different areas of the world, including your world, to line things up so that His will and His way will be found and walked.

As you begin to pray today, believe that God is already working on a meanwhile for you. He is taking steps, working things out, so that only good will come to you. If you are waiting, your God is working. Even if you don't see His hand, it's there.

This week, you'll be encountering five different "meanwhile" situations. May each build up your faith, increase your hope, and strengthen your prayers.

MEANWHILE, THE MIDIANITES

Jacob tore his clothes, put sackcloth around his waist,
and mourned for his son many days. . . . Meanwhile,
the Midianites sold Joseph in Egypt to Potiphar.

GENESIS 37:34, 36 HCSB

Poor Jacob. He'd just been given Joseph's multicolored dream coat, the one Jacob had given him for a gift, bloody and tattered. "A vicious animal has devoured him. Joseph has been torn to pieces!" (Genesis 37:33 HCSB). What other conclusion could Jacob reach?

Little did the mourning Jacob know that his favorite son, Joseph, was not dead. That he'd instead been sold by his own brothers to some traders. From there, the seventeen-year-old would become an Egyptian guard's slave, a man falsely accused of rape, a dungeon dweller, a dream interpreter, and, in the end, the number two man in Egypt, second only to Pharaoh. And from here, at age thirty-nine, Joseph would save the lives of his brothers and his father.

Only God can see the truth of each situation and the motives of each person's heart. No matter what you are shown or see to the contrary, know that God cares for you. He holds all your answers. You can trust Him with everything and everyone. So don't worry, mourn, or fear. God is already busy working things out. You'll see.

I know You have a plan, Lord. And in that and You I trust.

MEANWHILE, MOSES

The Israelites groaned. . . . God heard their groaning, and
He remembered His covenant with Abraham, Isaac, and Jacob.
God saw the Israelites, and He took notice. Meanwhile, Moses was
shepherding the flock of his father-in-law Jethro, the priest of Midian.

Exodus 2:23–3:1 HCSB

For centuries the Israelites had been enslaved in Egypt. So God raised up Moses. He made sure Moses had the best birth parents (from the house of Levi) and adoptive parent (Pharaoh's daughter). Things were going swimmingly, but then. . .

When Moses was all grown up, he saw a fellow Hebrew being beaten by an Egyptian. So Moses killed the aggressor. When his deed became known, he ran off to Midian where he stayed for forty years, married, and shepherded his father-in-law's sheep.

When the old pharaoh died, the Israelites groaned and moaned to God because of their enslavement. God heard their cries and remembered His promise to them. And so He went to talk to Moses via a burning bush.

God hears your cries, your prayers, your pleas. So when things look hopeless, don't despair. Know that God is in the midst of coordinating a rescue plan for you. Just keep the faith and keep praying, assured He's already working on your meanwhile.

God, please hear my prayer. Work Your plan.

MEANWHILE, THE CLOUD OF THE LORD

*They set out from the mountain of the LORD on a three-day journey
with the ark of the LORD's covenant traveling ahead of them for those
three days to seek a resting place for them. Meanwhile, the cloud of
the LORD was over them by day when they set out from the camp.*

NUMBERS 10:33–34 HCSB

If you think you might be walking alone, think again. God is not only
going ahead of you, scouting out a resting place, but also hovering
over you right now, where you sit, stand, or lie. Your Lord is making
sure you're safe, protected, and provided for.

The cloud of the Lord is a sign of His presence. The fact that
He not only goes before you but protects you wherever you are is
evidence that His power, presence, and protection are everywhere
you are and everywhere you aren't.

Why not, like Moses, recognize God going before you by saying/
praying, "Get up, GOD! Put down your enemies! Chase those who
hate you to the hills!" And when your day's traveling is over, say/pray,
"Rest with us, GOD, stay with the many, many thousands of Israel"
(Numbers 10:35–36 MSG).

*Thank You, Lord, for always being there for me, guiding,
leading, protecting, providing. You are my all in all!*

MEANWHILE, THE EGYPTIANS

On the day after the Passover the Israelites went
out triumphantly in the sight of all the Egyptians.
Meanwhile, the Egyptians were burying every firstborn
male the LORD had struck down among them.

NUMBERS 33:3–4 HCSB

God commanded Moses to keep a record of the Israelites' "start-
ing places of their travels" (Numbers 33:2 NLV). And thank God
He did. For Moses' notes, records, songs, history, and genealo-
gies are a wonderful resource for us. Moses' first five books of the
Bible—Genesis, Exodus, Leviticus, Numbers, and Deuteronomy—
are called the Pentateuch. Those writings give us insight
into what God was doing, how He worked His will in the world
through His Word, His power, and His strength.

It's amazing how the tide had turned for the Egyptians. How,
through His acts and words, God worked things out so that God's
children not only gained their freedom from their cruel overseers,
but also left Egypt with plunder, as instructed by God, taking with
them silver and gold jewelry, along with clothing (Exodus 12:35–36)!

Today, remember that God has things under control. While He's
helping you with one hand, He's hobbling your enemies and crushing
your obstacles with the other. All prayer and praise to Him!

Lord, I am so glad You have everything under
control. In that truth I trust and rest. Amen.

OPEN MOUTHS

*When they came up out of the water, the Spirit
of the Lord carried Philip away. . . . Meanwhile,
Saul was still breathing threats and murder
against the disciples of the Lord.*
ACTS 8:39; 9:1 HCSB

At the end of Acts 8, an angel of the Lord told the apostle Philip to get on a desert road and follow it to an Ethiopian eunuch. Philip obeyed. Once he found the eunuch, the Spirit told him to join the eunuch in his chariot, where he was reading from a scroll of Isaiah. Philip once again obeyed and helped the eunuch understand what he was reading. When the man asked to be baptized, Philip acquiesced. Then, when they came back out of the water, the Spirit carried Philip away.

In the beginning of Acts 9, Saul is breathing out threats and murder against people of the Way. While he's on the road to Damascus, Saul, blinded by a flash from heaven, has an uncomfortable encounter with Jesus.

On one side we have Philip obeying an angel and the Spirit. When he opened *his* mouth, the good news of Jesus came out (Acts 8:35). Meanwhile, Saul breathed threats and murder.

Consider your thoughts and words as you think and pray. What comes out when you open *your* mouth?

*May my thoughts, words, and prayers
reflect Your light and strength, Jesus.*

→ DATE:

Dear Heavenly Father, ...

....

....

....

....

Thank You for. . . ..

....

....

....

....

....

....

....

....

I am worried about. . . ..

....

....

....

....

....

PEOPLE I AM PRAYING FOR TODAY. . . ..

....

....

....

....

....

Here's what's happening in my life. . .

I need. . .

OTHER THINGS ON MY HEART THAT
I NEED TO SHARE WITH YOU, GOD. . .

Amen.
Thank You, Father,
for hearing my prayers.

At the Heart of the Matter

*"A man looks at the outside of a person,
but the Lord looks at the heart."*
1 Samuel 16:7 NLV

. . . .

God values your heart. He looks at it, into the core of your being, to determine the strength of your feelings, the truth of your words, the meaning of your thoughts, and the measure of your faith. Unlike humans with their limited abilities, God can reach the deep recesses within you to determine who you really and truly are.

Yet for some reason, you might still think you can hide something from God, the Creator, the supernatural, all-powerful, all-knowing, all-encompassing being. But you can't! No one can conceal anything from God. He has the x-ray glasses! His hearing is better than your mom's! And because God lives in the past, present, and future, He already knows and has already seen all you've done, said, and thought yesterday, all you're doing, saying, and thinking in this moment, and all you will do, say, and think tomorrow! So as much as you'd like to think you're hiding something from God, think again. Father God has His eyes on you!

Because God puts so much value on your heart and its inner recesses, you would be wise to spend some time looking at what role your heart is playing in your praying. Let's turn the page and begin!

AN INNER YOU

*"Do not look at the way he looks on the outside or how
tall he is, because I have not chosen him. For the Lord
does not look at the things man looks at. A man looks at
the outside of a person, but the Lord looks at the heart."*

1 SAMUEL 16:7 NLV

Unhappy with Saul, God's first choice for king, God told Samuel to go to Jesse because He would be providing a king from among his sons. So Samuel the prophet went.

Seeing Eliab, the eldest son, Samuel thought for sure he'd be the one God chose. But God told Samuel not to let appearances sway him.

After seven sons passed before Samuel, he asked Jesse if he had any more. Jesse replied yes, one more. David. He was out tending the sheep.

As it turned out, David was the Lord's chosen. And when Samuel anointed him, "the Spirit of the Lord came upon David with strength from that day on" (1 Samuel 16:13 NLV).

At times, God's answer to your prayers may lead you to interact with or pray for people you might not think worthy. Allow those thoughts to pass. Instead, trust God. He's heart smart.

*Guide me in Your wisdom, Lord. I want to take Your
lead when it comes to matters of the heart.*

HEART SMART

Keep my message in plain view at all times. Concentrate!
Learn it by heart! Those who discover these words live,
really live; body and soul, they're bursting with health. Keep
vigilant watch over your heart; that's where life starts.

PROVERBS 4:21–23 MSG

. . . .

To the Hebrews, the heart was the core of a person's being. It contained all that individual's knowledge and was consulted whenever decisions were to be made. The heart was who a person truly was, the real him or her that guided decisions and directed thoughts and emotions. It still is.

Being such an important component of who you are, your heart *must* be guarded from attack—above all other things! To protect your heart and yourself, be sure to have God's word plainly in view all the time. Focus on it. Understand it. Memorize it. Then, with God's Word etched on your heart, you will truly be living the life God created you to live! You'll be bursting with health from head to toe, inside and out.

Today, guard your heart by etching a verse onto it. Perhaps begin with John 14:1 (HCSB): "Your heart must not be troubled. Believe in God; believe also in Me."

Because I believe in You, Lord, my heart is unshaken.

NO DOUBT

"If anyone says to this mountain, 'Be lifted up and thrown into the sea,' and does not doubt in his heart, but believes that what he says will happen, it will be done for him. Therefore I tell you, all the things you pray and ask for—believe that you have received them, and you will have them."

MARK 11:23–24 HCSB

Jesus knew the importance of your heart, how whatever you plant in it will flow out of it. That's why He told you to "have faith in God [*constantly*]" (Mark 11:22 AMPC, emphasis added). To never doubt. Why? Because if you do not doubt in your heart, you can say to any mountain (any obstacle, any challenge), "Rise up and jump in the ocean," and it will happen. What you ask for, what you request, what you pray for will be answered, given, delivered!

Today, make an effort to faithfully practice Jesus' prayer formula. As you pray, do not doubt in your heart but believe that what you say will happen. When you ask God for something—and that something is in His will for you—believe you have already received it. And you will!

Lord, help me to pray and follow You more faithfully by harboring no doubts in my heart but continually believing You in all things.

WHOLEHEARTED PRAYER

Jesus said, "The first in importance is, 'Listen, Israel:
The Lord your God is one; so love the Lord God with all
your passion and prayer and intelligence and energy.' And
here is the second: 'Love others as well as you love yourself.'
There is no other commandment that ranks with these."

MARK 12:29–31 MSG

A scribe, who was usually a supporter of chief priests and Jewish elders, asked Jesus what the most important commandment was. Jesus, who knew the Bible by heart, responded in part by quoting Deuteronomy 6:4–5, telling the scribe a person was to love God with all her heart, soul, mind, and strength. The second commandment Jesus quoted was from Leviticus 19:18: love your neighbor as yourself. All the other commandments would be satisfied if these two were obeyed.

Interestingly, *The Message* translates these verses differently than all the other versions of the Bible. *The Message* author Eugene Peterson is inviting you to have a different perspective. Today, love God with all your soul. Offer that love by using the gift and powers of prayer from the depths of your soul. Begin today.

Lord, I love You more than anything in this world.
You are my heart, strength, and power. Today,
I offer You prayers of love from the depths of my soul.

CENTERED AND DEVOTED

*"Let your heart be completely devoted to the L*ORD *our God to walk in His statutes and to keep His commands, as it is today."*
1 KINGS 8:61 HCSB

. . . .

Solomon, the wisest king ever (1 Kings 10:23), said the words above to his people when he was praying over the temple he had built for God. Solomon wanted the people of Israel to know that Yahweh was the one and only God. The Lord's followers should be focused on Him alone. Thus, their hearts were to be completely devoted to God.

Solomon was right. Yet you might be wondering to yourself, *How can I get there from here? How can I go from being majorly distracted by the world to being totally focused on God alone?* Solomon provides the answer: "May GOD. . .continue to be with us just as he was with our ancestors—may he never give up and walk out on us. May he keep us centered and devoted to him, following the life path he has cleared, watching the signposts, walking at the pace and rhythms he laid down for our ancestors" (1 Kings 8:57–58 MSG).

God has all things carefully planned out, your life included. So don't freak out. Just get focused. Do so by allowing God to keep you centered on Him.

Walk with me, Lord. Help me center my life on You.

→ DATE:

Dear Heavenly Father, ...

....

....

....

....

Thank You for. . ...

....

....

....

....

....

....

....

I am worried about. . ...

....

....

....

....

....

....

PEOPLE I AM PRAYING FOR TODAY. . ...

....

....

....

....

....

Here's what's happening in my life. . .

....

....

....

....

I need. . .

....

....

....

....

....

....

....

....

....

....

....

....

....

....

....

....

....

....

OTHER THINGS ON MY HEART THAT
I NEED TO SHARE WITH YOU, GOD. . .

....

....

....

....

....

....

....

....

amen.
Thank You, Father,
for hearing my prayers.

God the All-Knowing One

Do you not know? Have you not heard? Yahweh is the everlasting God, the Creator of the whole earth. He never grows faint or weary; there is no limit to His understanding.
ISAIAH 40:28 HCSB

• •

When you're confused, when you don't know which way to turn, when you begin to lose your way, when you're down to your last dime, when you're out of strength and energy, go to God. Pray to Yahweh. He's always around, has been around forever. Literally.

God, the most powerful being in your life, is tireless. No one and nothing can compare to Him in energy, strength, wisdom, or power. Because God created and sustains all things in and out of this world, His taking care of you is relatively easy. And He'll never stop doing it.

Your Father God is one "parent" who will always be around to guide, protect, help, and advise you. He will never not take your calls or hang up on you. But most importantly, God understands you. He knows you like a book, one He's read from cover to cover, over and over again. He is watching, waiting, and working to help you live your purpose.

This week's readings will center on prayers to the One who gets you like no one else. The One you can pray to 24-7. The One who never sleeps. The One who says, "Speak, child. I'm listening."

HIGH ROCK

Hear my cry, O God. Listen to my prayer. I call to You from the end of the earth when my heart is weak. Lead me to the rock that is higher than I. For You have been a safe place for me, a tower of strength where I am safe.

PSALM 61:1–3 NLV

God knows there will be days when you have no strength. When your heart is weak, your balance off, your legs shaky, He'll be there, waiting to hear your prayer, to hear you admit—to yourself and Him—that you need His help.

When the psalmist talks of God leading him "to the rock that is higher than I," he's admitting there are some difficulties he cannot overcome without divine assistance, some places he cannot reach without God's boost up.

It's okay to admit you need God, to leave yourself in His hands, to let Him bear all your burdens. He's the shoulder you can cry on, the God you can pray to, the Father you can rely on, the Companion you can sit beside.

Today, ask God to lend you an ear. To pull you up and over to His high rock. Allow Him to watch over you as you enter that safe place, that tower of strength.

"God. . .when I'm far from anywhere, down to my last gasp, I call out, 'Guide me up High Rock Mountain!'" (Psalm 61:1–2 MSG).

147

GOD ONLY KNOWS

It so happened that after Pharaoh released the people, God didn't lead them by the road through the land of the Philistines, which was the shortest route, for God thought, "If the people encounter war, they'll change their minds and go back to Egypt."

EXODUS 13:17 MSG

Pharaoh had finally okayed the Israelites' exit, and God was ready to get them out of Egypt safely. Yet He knew that at this early stage they weren't the most confident and courageous crowd. If He took them the shortest route, chances were they'd meet up with enemies prepared for battle. So God decided to take them the long way around, through the wilderness and across the Red Sea.

Yet at the same time, God wanted His people to be able to continue to witness His power and strength. What better way than to lead them to a place where He'd have to divide a great sea, keep a path open for them to cross, then bring back the waters to drown their enemy!

Just as God knew the strengths and weaknesses of the Israelites, He knows yours. Be assured, God will take you by the best route, the one He's already staked out for you.

Lead me Your way, Lord.

GOD KNOWS YOUR WAY

Although my spirit is weak within me, You know my way.
Along this path I travel they have hidden a trap for me. Look
to the right and see: no one stands up for me; there is no refuge
for me; no one cares about me. I cry to You, Lord; I say, "You
are my shelter, my portion in the land of the living."

PSALM 142:3–5 HCSB

. . . .

Containing only seven verses, Psalm 142 was written by David when
he was in a cave. As a whole, the psalm is described as a prayer.

The shepherd boy who fought and defeated lions, wolves, bears,
and giants, and later became a king, was apparently in a dark place.
Yet no matter how bleak David's circumstances, how dark his situation, or how weak his spirit, he was certain of one thing: God knew
David's every step, location, plan, idea, thought. He knew where all
the traps lay along the way for the apple of His eye.

When you are weak, in a dark place, or amid unpleasant circumstances, take heart. Know that God knows where you are. He
will shelter you where you are, then lead you out by the nearest exit.

Lord, You are my shelter. May You always know
my way and meet me wherever I land.

149

SHEPHERD, STRENGTH, AND SHIELD

*The Lord is my strength and my safe cover. My heart trusts in Him,
and I am helped. So my heart is full of joy. . . . The Lord is the strength
of His people. He is a safe place. . . . Save Your people and bring
good to what is Yours. Be their shepherd and carry them forever.*

PSALM 28:7–9 NLV

. . . .

There may be days when you aren't sure of your way. The path ahead
is shadowy at best. You're a bit tired, confused, feeling vulnerable.
You know you can't go back but feel you need help where you stand,
right now, in this moment.

No need to panic. Just head back to the Rock. You know His love
for you, how kind He's always been. It's time to start waving your
hands, getting His attention, calling out for some supernatural help.

Today, remember who Your strength and shield is: God. He's
the Shepherd you can cry out to, call, no matter where you are. His
ears are attuned to your voice. He will give you the strength you
need, the shelter you long for. Just continue to trust in Him alone.
For He's doesn't just *know* your way; He *is* the Way and carries you
along with Him. Forever.

Lift me up to You, Lord. Carry me forever in Your arms.

GIVING WAY TO THE LORD

Trust in the Lord, and do good. So you will live in the land and will be fed. Be happy in the Lord. And He will give you the desires of your heart. Give your way over to the Lord. Trust in Him also. And He will do it.

PSALM 37:3–5 NLV

God doesn't only *know* your way. He's waiting for you to *give* your way over to Him. He wants you to trust Him *all* the way.

There may be some secret desires in your heart that you have yet to share with God—perhaps even share with yourself. Perhaps you think the enormity of your dreams or desires seems too much to contemplate, plan out, or take on. If so, it may be time to reconsider your vision of God. For there is nothing—no problem, no dream, no desire, no impossibility—that is bigger than your all-powerful Lord, Creator, and Savior. God can do anything and will do anything, will grant any desire that is in His will for you. For those are the only desires worthy of your time and attention.

Today as you pray, hand over to God *all* the desires of your heart. Trust Him to work them into His will and your way.

Lord, here are my desires and my way,
from my heart and hands to Yours.

→ DATE:

Dear Heavenly Father, ...

....

....

....

....

Thank You for. . . ..

....

....

....

....

....

....

....

....

I am worried about. . . ..

....

....

....

....

....

PEOPLE I AM PRAYING FOR TODAY. . . ..

....

....

....

....

....

Here's what's happening in my life. . .

I need. . .

OTHER THINGS ON MY HEART THAT
I NEED TO SHARE WITH YOU, GOD. . .

Amen.
Thank You, Father,
for hearing my prayers.

God Makes a Way

*It is God who is working in you, enabling you both
to desire and to work out His good purpose.*
PHILIPPIANS 2:13 HCSB

No matter how impossible the odds, how unlikely the solution, how vague the process, you can always count on one thing. God *will* make a way for you through the forest, even when all you can see is the tree in front of you.

The fact that God will help you find a way through any and every situation you might encounter is an extremely important precept to keep in mind when all you can see are your own solutions or when God seems distant and His answers, at best, obscure.

As a follower of God, you must have faith He hears your prayers. While waiting for an answer, you must keep an open mind and heart, because chances are that what God sees as a solution is very different from the answer you had in mind.

In this week's readings, you'll see some prayers, complaints, and cries that were lifted up to God, *and* the solutions that He came up with to address and answer those prayers, perhaps far beyond what the petitioners ever imagined. And why not? He's the unfathomable God who always supplies the right answer in the lives of His dear children.

PARTING THE RED SEA

"Do not be afraid! Be strong, and see how the Lord will save you today. For the Egyptians you have seen today, you will never see again. The Lord will fight for you. All you have to do is keep still."

EXODUS 14:13–14 NLV

Leaving Pharaoh and centuries of bondage behind, the Israelites had walked out of Egypt. But God decided not to take them the shortcut, through Philistine territory and into the Promised Land. For "the people may change their minds when they see war, and return to Egypt" (Exodus 13:17 NLV).

So God led them into the wilderness, toward the Red Sea. But soon Pharaoh, regretting his decision to let God's people go, chased after them with his army of chariots.

When God's children saw the approaching army, they cried out to God for help. But Moses told them God would save them. And He did. He parted the sea, allowing His children to cross to the other side. Once they were safely on the far shore, He brought the water back over the Egyptian army.

Maybe your situation isn't as dire as the Israelites'. But that doesn't mean it's any less important. Just remember to keep your faith and courage. Pray. And God will make a way.

Lord, I need Your help. Please make a way for me—in You!

155

AN INVISIBLE AND UNTRACEABLE SHEPHERD

*Your way [in delivering Your people] was through the sea,
and Your paths through the great waters, yet Your footsteps
were not traceable, but were obliterated. You led Your
people like a flock by the hand of Moses and Aaron.*

PSALM 77:19–20 AMPC

You, a solidly visible, earthbound creature, have faith in a God who is not just supernatural and invisible but also untraceable. You, who can see and be seen, trust a God who can see but remains unseen.

For you, like the psalmist, know God hears your cries. During the day of trouble, you seek out God. Then in the night hours, your hand is "stretched out [in prayer] without slacking up" (Psalm 77:2 AMPC).

It's only with the eyes and ears of faith that you can see and hear your Creator. You know for certain that because you trust Him, all will work out in the end. No matter how things look today. No matter how deep the waters get. All you have to do is remember to walk in His will and way. To walk forward even though you don't see God or His footprints upon your path.

Lead me by the hand, Good Shepherd. Help me cross this sea.

TESTING, TESTING, TESTING

*"When you hit the rock, water will come out
of it and the people will drink."*
EXODUS 17:6 NLV

. . . .

For some people, no matter how many times a miracle is worked in front of them, still they doubt, fear, complain, and moan to whoever will listen.

In this particular situation, Moses is leading the Israelites through the wilderness, stage by stage. When they camped at Rephidim, the people started complaining to Moses, saying, "Give us water to drink" (Exodus 17:2 HCSB). Moses asked, "Why are you complaining to me about it? And while I'm at it, I might as well ask, why do you keep testing God?" Yet still Moses' thirsty crowd whined and moaned, saying things like, "Why didn't God just kill us in Egypt instead of bringing us and our families out here to die of thirst?"

Finally, "Moses cried out in prayer to GOD" (17:4 MSG), asking Him what he could do with these people. That's when God came up with a unique solution. He told Moses to hit a rock at Horeb. Water would come out of it and the people's thirst would be quenched. Moses hit the rock. Water came. The people drank.

Don't moan. Don't groan. Don't test. Don't wrest. Just pray. God will find a way.

I need help, Lord. Show me the way, what to pray.

WHICH WAY?

Thomas said to Jesus, "Lord, we do not know where
You are going. How can we know the way to get there?"
Jesus said, "I am the Way and the Truth and the Life.
No one can go to the Father except by Me."

JOHN 14:5–6 NLV

What do you do when you don't know what to do? Where do you go when you don't know where to go? That's what Thomas, one of Jesus' twelve disciples, wanted to know. Speaking for all twelve, Thomas told Jesus they didn't know where He was going, nor how to get there. So Jesus made it simple. He said He was the Way, the Truth, and the Life. All they needed to do was follow Him. Then they would never be lost.

So, child of God, when you're looking for the Way, the first thing to do is take note of where you are now. What are you doing? Are you following hard after Jesus, eyes and ears open to His will and way, or have you veered off His path and started carving out your own way? Today, take stock and look for His way.

I'm looking for You and Your way, Lord.
Tell me. . .which way, Lord? Which way?

A STRANGE WAY

Because he did not give the glory to God. . .
he became infected with worms and died.
Then God's message flourished and multiplied.

ACTS 12:23–24 HCSB

· ·

When Herod realized how pleased the Jews were at the killing of the disciple James, he had Peter arrested and put him in jail under guard. Later, after Passover, Peter would be handed over to the people.

So to prison Peter went and to prayer went the church (Acts 12:5). The kind of praying the church did is described as fervent and persistent (AMPC), earnest (ESV), and most strenuous (MSG). The result? An angel appeared in the jail cell. He woke Peter up. The disciple's chains fell off and before he knew it, he was standing in front of the house where the church had been praying.

When Herod found out about the escape, he searched for Peter but to no avail. Soon after, when a crowd yelled that his voice was "of a god, not of a man" (Acts 12:22 NLV), the king "did not give the glory to God." So the angel of the Lord stopped Herod's words forever. Yet God's message flourished.

Today, pray that God would work to find you a way. Then follow *His* lead, no matter how strange.

I want my way to align with Yours, Lord.
Help me to follow Your lead!

→ DATE:

Dear Heavenly Father, ...

....

....

....

....

Thank You for. . . ..

....

....

....

....

....

....

....

....

I am worried about. . . ..

....

....

....

....

....

....

PEOPLE I AM PRAYING FOR TODAY. . . ..

....

....

....

....

....

Here's what's happening in my life. . .

I need. . .

OTHER THINGS ON MY HEART THAT
I NEED TO SHARE WITH YOU, GOD. . .

amen.
Thank You, Father,
for hearing my prayers.

Keep Well

Beloved, I pray that you may prosper in every way and [that your body] may keep well, even as [I know] your soul keeps well and prospers.
3 JOHN 2 AMPC

· ·

God thinks about you night and day. He has plans for your life, plans for your "welfare and peace and not for evil, to give you hope in your final outcome" (Jeremiah 29:11 AMPC). He wants you to have a life of plenty. And Jesus is proof of that truth, saying, "I came that they may have and enjoy life, and have it in abundance (to the full, till it overflows)" (John 10:10 AMPC).

Jesus is your Good Shepherd, the One willing and wanting to lay down His life for you. He's your go-to Man for all you need in this life and the next. He's your guard and guide, your wisdom and courage, your strength and song. Jesus is all you need in heaven and on earth.

Whatever malady you may be suffering, God's Son is your remedy. Jesus is the mother who nurses you, the shepherd who guides you, the friend who sticks by you, the teacher who instructs you, the brother who lays down His life for you, and the physician who heals you.

This week you'll see how throughout the ages, God has been working in the lives of His people, desiring them to be prosperous followers of Him in body, soul, spirit, and mind forever.

LIFTED UP

As Moses lifted up the snake in the desert, so the
Son of Man must be lifted up. Then whoever puts his
trust in Him will have life that lasts forever.

JOHN 3:14–15 NLV

Toward the end of their wilderness journey, the Israelites once more lost their patience with God. They wanted real food and water, no more of this manna from heaven.

So God's children complained to Moses, again! People who'd witnessed so many miracles of God, so much of His power, were whining. For along with those miracles, they'd endured trial after trial. Tired of their wanderings, the Israelites said they'd rather be slaves in Egypt than live free in the wilderness with God.

The Israelites' ungratefulness was palpable. So God took action, sending poisonous snakes among His children. Many died. And once more they went to Moses, this time contrite, pleading for him to pray to God to take the serpents away! So Moses prayed, and God provided a bronze snake. Anyone who'd been bitten could look at it and live.

Just as Moses lifted up the snake so that the people could live, Jesus was lifted up so that you can live (John 3:14–15). Look up. Live.

I'm looking to You, Jesus, for life and health. In You
I trust, to You I pray, and in You I live. Amen.

THE CENTERED HEART

Listen to my words. Turn your ear to my sayings. Do not let them leave your eyes. Keep them in the center of your heart. For they are life to those who find them, and healing to their whole body.

PROVERBS 4:20–22 NLV

. . . .

If you're looking for wisdom, for a way to live your life for God, open your eyes, ears, mind, heart, soul, and spirit to Proverbs' divinely inspired words. Actually listen to God's words of wisdom (aka WOWs); heed them. Write them on the projection screen of your mind and keep your eyes fixed on them. For there you will find the power not just to live but to stay healthy and in line with what God would have you do and be. For at the center of your heart and life, at the foundation of all you say and do, will be the good news of Jesus Christ.

Today, start at the beginning. Make it your intention to attend to God's wisdom, word by word, sentence by sentence, precept by precept. Memorize those verses, phrases, or words that speak to you the most. Keep them close. For as you do so, as you draw near to God, He'll draw near to you.

*Help me, Lord, as my ears open to Your voice and
my heart centers on Your healing words.*

STEPS

Naaman went down and dipped himself in the Jordan seven times, according to the command of the man of God. Then his skin was restored and became like the skin of a small boy, and he was clean.

2 KINGS 5:14 HCSB

Naaman, a commander of the Syrian army, was not only a brave fighter but also, to his dismay, a leper. On one of the Syrians' raids, the soldiers brought back a little girl from Israel who became the maid of Naaman's wife. Seeing her master's skin problems, the girl told her mistress about the prophet Elisha. She thought for sure he could heal Naaman.

So Naaman went to visit Elisha. But Elisha didn't even invite Naaman inside! He just sent a messenger to the door, telling Naaman to wash seven times in the Jordan. But this proud commander couldn't understand why Elisha wouldn't just come to the door, wave his hand, and heal Naaman. So he stomped off. Later, his servants helped him to see reason. Naaman finally followed Elisha's directions and was healed—immediately!

When you need healing, going to God is the first step. And the second is to follow His directions, no matter how outlandish or humbling they may seem at the time.

*I need Your healing touch, Lord.
Show me what to do and I will do it.*

PRAYER PARTNERS

*Are you hurting? Pray. Do you feel great? Sing. Are you
sick? Call the church leaders together to pray and anoint
you with oil in the name of the Master. Believing-prayer will
heal you, and Jesus will put you on your feet. And if you've
sinned, you'll be forgiven—healed inside and out.*

JAMES 5:13–15 MSG

One way to increase your prayer power for healing is to ask others to pray
with and for you. Instead of giving in to the anxiety, negative mind-
set, and frustration that illness sometimes brings with it, allow your
church elders and others to get together and pray over you and to
anoint you with oil in Jesus' name.

God's Son cures all things. Just by being in His presence, you
are nourished and nurtured. Just by being near Him, you will find
yourself renewed, at peace, and safe.

The healing you're looking for may not be for physical illness
but some other malady that is bringing you down, keeping you from
being the woman God created you to be. But thank God, Jesus can
heal every kind of sickness.

Today, consider asking someone strong in faith to pray for your
healing, if the Spirit so leads. But if you're feeling better, why not
sing instead?

Lord, be with me. Lay Your healing touch upon me.

GOD, THE LIGHT BEARER

*Those who are right with the Lord cry, and He hears them.
And He takes them from all their troubles. The Lord is near to
those who have a broken heart. And He saves those who are
broken in spirit. A man who does what is right and good may
have many troubles. But the Lord takes him out of them all.*

PSALM 34:17–19 NLV

Sometimes it may be difficult to understand why some people are divinely delivered of their maladies and others are not. But the important thing to remember is that no matter where you stand health wise, whether healed or hurting, God is with you. He has heard your pleas and your prayers. And you can rest assured your loving Father God will take away all the troubles weighing you down.

When your heart is breaking, God is closer than the tear streaming down your cheek. When you feel like you can't go on, God comes alongside and carries you. When all you see is darkness, God will bring the light. Woman, do your best. And leave the rest to the Lord.

*Shine Your light on my pathway, Lord. Heal my
fractured spirit. Pull me close to You.*

167

→ DATE:

Dear Heavenly Father, ...

....

....

....

....

Thank You for. . . ..

....

....

....

....

....

....

....

....

I am worried about. . . ..

....

....

....

....

....

PEOPLE I AM PRAYING FOR TODAY. . . ..

....

....

....

....

....

Here's what's happening in my life. . . ..

....

....

....

....

I need. . ...

....

....

....

....

....

....

....

....

....

....

....

....

....

....

....

....

....

OTHER THINGS ON MY HEART THAT I NEED TO SHARE WITH YOU, GOD. . .

....

....

....

....

....

....

....

....

Amen.
Thank You, Father,
for hearing my prayers.

Prayer, the Doorway to God's Presence

*God said, "My presence will go with you.
I'll see the journey to the end."*
EXODUS 33:14 MSG

Sometimes God sends His angels or human compadres to help you fight your battles or to scout out the land that lies ahead of you. Other times you may not want or need anyone but God with you, helping you find your way, for only His presence will give you the strength and confidence to do what He's calling you to do.

That's how Moses felt when God told him He'd be sending His angel to drive out the Israelites enemies (Exodus 33:2). So Moses prayed to his friend God face-to-face, saying, "I pray to You, if I have found favor in Your eyes, let me know Your ways. Then I may know You and find favor in Your eyes" (Exodus 33:13 NLV). God responded by assuring Moses, "My presence will go with you. I'll see the journey to the end" (Exodus 33:14 MSG).

Sometimes God Himself is the only One who can fulfill your desires and help you find your way. He promises to provide you with everything you need. Today and every day, pray your way into God's presence, talking with Him as a friend, one on one. Allow Him full sway in your life and He'll see your journey to the end.

STRAINING TO HEAR

God's there, listening for all who pray, for all who pray and mean it. He does what's best for those who fear him—hears them call out, and saves them. God sticks by all who love him.

PSALM 145:18–20 MSG

Wondering where God has been, is now, or will be? Look no further. For David's psalm of praise says that God is right there with you, His ear turned toward you. He's waiting for you to speak, unload all your troubles, tell Him all your dreams and desires. But God isn't a fan of surface prayers. For He wants you to look deep within yourself. To pray with your whole self, meaning each word you utter.

For those who honor, obey, and love Him, God will do what's best. Straining to hear even your slightest whisper of a prayer, God is ready and willing to save you. To stand by you because of His overwhelming affection for you.

Today, meditate on the God who sticks by you when no one else will, the One who listens when others have turned away. Pray your way into His presence, knowing you never need to worry about anything because your God knows and does what's best.

Lord, I'm going deep as I pray today. Hear my words. . . .

GOD IN ACTION

"When two of you get together on anything at all on earth and make a prayer of it, my Father in heaven goes into action. And when two or three of you are together because of me, you can be sure that I'll be there."

MATTHEW 18:19–20 MSG

Sometimes you may feel as if you cannot move heaven and earth. Yet technically you can—because you can move the Mover.

In today's verses, Jesus tells His followers that there's power in numbers. If two believers get together and pray in accordance with God's will, He will go into action! And while you're there with God together, Jesus is sure to be there as well!

It all sounds so amazing. That God, the Lord of all creation, is moved by your prayers, pleas, petitions, and praises when you and at least one other believer come to Him with an issue, a problem, a worry, a hope, a longing, a desire. Like any good father, God cares about you. He wants you to know that He sees you, He knows what you're struggling with, and He wants to help. He longs to help.

Today, consider sharing a concern with another believer. Then ask if they will be so good as to pray with you.

We feel Your presence among us, Lord.
Open Your ears to our prayer.

JESUS THE DOOR

*I am the Door; anyone who enters in through Me
will be saved (will live). He will come in and he
will go out [freely], and will find pasture.*

JOHN 10:9 AMPC

Jesus is the door or gateway into the sheepfold. Only through Him can believers find entry into God's presence and kingdom. Only through Jesus will you be saved and find the provisions you need to do what God calls you to do and live as He calls you to live.

Yet to know where to access Jesus, how to reach Him, no matter how early or late the hour, you must be able to hear and later recognize His voice. For you don't want to follow any old shepherd. You want to follow Jesus. He alone holds the key to your life and future.

The best way to get familiar with Jesus' voice is to read His Father's Word. Only then will you be able to discern the Good Shepherd's will and way from all others. Only then will you be able to discern the path He would have you take.

As you pray your way into God's presence and spend some one-on-one time with Him today, imprint His voice upon your mind, etch His words upon your heart. Get to know Him as He knows you.

*Good Shepherd, in Your presence I long to
be. Please speak. I'm listening.*

CLOSER THAN IMAGINED

"He made from one blood all nations who live on the earth.
He set the times and places where they should live.
They were to look for God. Then they might feel after Him
and find Him because He is not far from each one of us.
It is in Him that we live and move and keep on living."

ACTS 17:26–28 NLV

Potential idols are everywhere. Wikipedia defines *idolatry* as "the worship of an idol or cult image, being a physical image, such as a statue, or a person in place of God."

In the Old Testament, idolatry ran rampant, even, at times, among God's own people (Exodus 32) and against God's clearly expressed and recorded commands (Exodus 20:3–4).

What you worship today might not be a golden calf. It may be your television set, smartphone, laptop, social status, or simply cold hard cash.

Today, consider what may have unseated God from the throne of your life. Then go to God in prayer. Ask Him to forgive your unintentional misstep and help you make it your daily intention to seek God, the One who's closer than you've ever imagined. And always will be.

You alone, Lord, are the One I worship. For in
You alone I live, move, and have my being.

WHO MOVED?

Be subject to God. Resist the devil [stand firm against him], and he will flee from you. Come close to God and He will come close to you.

JAMES 4:7–8 AMPC

There will be times in your life when you find yourself wondering what happened to God. You begin asking yourself questions like *Where could God be? Doesn't He see what's happening in my life?* That's when you might want to consider that perhaps you're feeling far away from God not because *He* moved but because *you* did.

Today, consider looking around. Take stock of where you're standing, what you're seeing. If all you see is trouble on the horizon with no place to turn, chances are there's some distance between you and your Maker. That's a signal to turn yourself, your hopes, your dreams, your thoughts, and your heart over to God. Shrug off the devil. Give him his walking papers, tell him to take a hike, whatever you have to do to put some spiritual miles between you and him. Then draw near to God through prayer. For as you draw closer to Him, He'll sidle up closer to you.

Here I am, Lord. To You I give myself and my hopes, dreams, thoughts, and heart.

→ DATE:

Dear Heavenly Father, ...

....

....

....

....

Thank You for. . . ..

....

....

....

....

....

....

....

....

I am worried about. . . ..

....

....

....

....

....

PEOPLE I AM PRAYING FOR TODAY. . . ..

....

....

....

....

....

Here's what's happening in my life. . . ..
....
....
....
....

I need. . ...

....

....

....

....

....

....

....

....

....

....

....

....

....

....

....

....

....

OTHER THINGS ON MY HEART THAT I NEED TO SHARE WITH YOU, GOD. . .

....

....

....

....

....

....

....

....

Amen.
Thank You, Father,
for hearing my prayers.

The Don'ts of Prayer

*Jesus had been praying. One of His followers
said to Him, "Lord, teach us to pray."*
LUKE 11:1 NLV

- -

Prayer, just like any other activity, has some dos and don'ts attached to it. Some of those don'ts were given to us directly by Jesus. Others were provided by His followers. All are to be heeded if you want to make your prayers as powerful and effective as possible. Yet even before tackling the dos and don'ts of prayer, the person praying must have the heart of a student and fully accept Jesus as her teacher.

Apparently, Jesus "often withdrew to deserted places and prayed" (Luke 5:16 HCSB). Six chapters later, in Luke 11, the disciples once again noticed Jesus praying. When He had finished His one-on-one with God, "one of His disciples said to Him, Lord, teach us to pray" (Luke 11:1 AMPC), and so He did, teaching His followers the Lord's Prayer.

During the next five days, imagine you are a new disciple of Jesus, knowing nothing about prayer. But you are ready, willing, open, and humble hearted enough to soak in Jesus' words, follow His directions, and gain new insights and attitudes regarding the most powerful tool in your box.

DON'T BE A HYPOCRITE

*"When you pray, do not be as those who pretend to be
someone they are not. They love to stand and pray in the places
of worship or in the streets so people can see them. For sure,
I tell you, they have all the reward they are going to get."*

MATTHEW 6:5 NLV

Back in Jesus' day, Jews would stand up in the synagogue or on the street corner and "perform" a prayer. They played up their pleas and praises, enjoying an audience around them as they staged their petitions to God.

The term Jesus used to describe these public petitioners was *hypocrites*. Interestingly enough, Merriam-Webster defines the term first as "a person who puts on a false appearance of virtue or religion" and second as "a person who acts in contradiction to his or her stated beliefs or feelings." Neither definition is one Jesus would want applied to you.

So if you're not to pray as a hypocrite, whose reward is his audience, how are you to pray? In a room. Alone. With the door shut. There you're to pray to your "Father who is in secret. And your Father who sees in secret will reward you" (Matthew 6:6 ESV).

*Alone with You, Lord, my eyes closed and
heart open, I pray. Dear Father. . .*

DON'T RATTLE ON

"When you pray, do not say the same thing over and over again making long prayers like the people who do not know God. They think they are heard because their prayers are long. Do not be like them."

MATTHEW 6:7–8 NLV

Have you ever fallen asleep while someone else was praying? Totally understandable. It has happened before. Chances are the person whose prayer rocked you to sleep was more interested in hearing her own voice and impressing others than humbly approaching God with her pleas and petitions.

The last thing God wants is for you to do all the talking or to go on and on and on about something. God, like most listeners really, wants to hear what you have to say. He is passionately interested in what is on your heart. But He'd rather have your prayers short and sweet. Direct and to the point.

When Peter began sinking in the stormy sea, thinking he was going to drown, he yelled to Jesus, "Lord, save me" (Matthew 14:30 ESV). Three little words. *Lord*, the one God to whom you submit yourself. *Save*, the action needed. *Me*, the object of that action.

Today, after you pray, consider the heart of your prayer. Which words (between three and seven) can you scale it down to?

Lord, lift me above this storm.

DON'T WAVER

Only it must be in faith that he asks with no wavering
(no hesitating, no doubting). For the one who wavers
(hesitates, doubts) is like the billowing surge out at sea
that is blown hither and thither and tossed by the wind.

JAMES 1:6 AMPC

When you pray to God, do you really believe that you will receive what you ask for? Or do you hesitate, perhaps believing your need may be bigger than your God?

Jesus sternly told His disciples, "I am telling you, whatever you ask for in prayer, believe (trust and be confident) that it is granted to you, and you will [get it]" (Mark 11:24 AMPC). In other words, Jesus wants each praying person to believe they've received what they're praying for in the moment in which they're praying for it—not when they actually do receive it! Jesus wants your faith to be there as you are asking!

If you've yet to put this point into practice, now's your chance. Today, consider your petitions before you pray. Then gather up all your faith and believe that you've received your request as you present it to God, without wavering or wandering in thought or deed.

Thank You, Lord, for answering my prayer,
for granting my request for. . .

DON'T BE SNOOTY

"If you walk around with your nose in the air, you're going to end up flat on your face, but if you're content to be simply yourself, you will become more than yourself."

LUKE 18:14 MSG

The last thing God wants is for you to come before Him with an attitude. That's why Jesus told the disciples the parable of the tax collector and the Pharisee, two men who went to the temple to pray. The Pharisee took pride in his morals. When he prayed, he thanked God he wasn't like other people, like criminals, adulterers, and tax collectors. He reminded the Lord (and anyone listening) how he fasted two times each week and tithed to the synagogue.

Then the tax collector, standing at a distance from the temple, prayed. Not able to lift his eyes to heaven, he asked God to have pity on him, a sinner. Jesus said that this second man, the one who humbled himself before God in prayer, was the one God would lift up, the one who would become what God created him to be.

Today as you pray, consider your attitude. Who are you closer to emulating—the Pharisee or the tax collector? What might you need to do to correct your course?

I come humbly before You, Lord, as a sinner whom You've made a saint. Forgive me!

DON'T GIVE UP

*Be earnest and unwearied and steadfast in your prayer
[life], being [both] alert and intent in [your praying] with
thanksgiving. And at the same time pray for us also,
that God may open a door to us for the Word.*

COLOSSIANS 4:2–3 AMPC

The apostle Paul made it clear to the Colossian believers what kind of prayer life they were to have. He wanted them to be devoted to praying. They were to stick with it, to stay alert, mindful, and ever watchful. To look for areas where prayer was needed. And not just to lift up their petitions but to pray with thankfulness—and to pray not only for themselves but for others.

When was the last time you thanked God for something? What did that something happen to be? Why did you single out that blessing and not another?

In the days ahead, live and pray with your eyes wide open to your needs and the needs of others. Try praying with the intention of thanking God for at least three things each day. Then consider praying for Christians everywhere, that God may use them to open doors for His Word.

*Help me, Lord, to be more alert to what and
who You would have me pray for.*

→ DATE:

Dear Heavenly Father, ...
....
....
....
....

Thank You for. . . ..
....
....
....
....
....
....
....
....

I am worried about. . . ..
....
....
....
....
....
....

PEOPLE I AM PRAYING FOR TODAY. . . ..
....
....
....
....
....

Here's what's happening in my life. . .

I need. . .

OTHER THINGS ON MY HEART THAT
I NEED TO SHARE WITH YOU, GOD. . .

Amen.
Thank You, Father,
for hearing my prayers.

The Do's of Prayer

*The earnest (heartfelt, continued) prayer of a righteous man
makes tremendous power available [dynamic in its working].*
JAMES 5:16 AMPC

. . . .

Along with all the don'ts of prayer, the Word of God provides you
with much advice to ensure that your prayers will be powerful and
effective. One of the main "to dos" is to live right with God. For
when you do, your prayers will be packed with power, a power to
be reckoned with.

The prophet Elijah had such power. He was a mere human, just
like you. Yet Elijah was also right with God. Thus, when Elijah prayed
very hard for no rain, it didn't rain. For three years. Then, as directed
by God, Elijah went back to Ahab. The prophet then prayed that it
would rain. Seven times "he bowed down on the ground and put his
face between his knees" (1 Kings 18:42 HCSB), prayed, then sent his
servant to go look toward the sea to see if he could discern any rain
forming. The first six times, the servant saw nothing. Yet the seventh
time, a cloud "as small as a man's hand" (18:44 HCSB) came in from
the sea, bringing loads of much-needed rain along with it.

In the next few days, consider how you can become more earnest
in prayer. Then get ready to use the divine strength that comes with
your newfound power.

NO MATTER WHAT

*Be cheerful no matter what; pray all the time; thank
God no matter what happens. This is the way God
wants you who belong to Christ Jesus to live.*

1 THESSALONIANS 5:16–18 MSG

Today's verses describe how God wants you to be. It sounds like a tall order, but if you look at each suggestion by itself, you'll find that all these things combine to make you powerful in prayer and your prayers a powerful tool.

When writing to the Thessalonian believers, Paul encouraged them to be cheerful—"no matter what." You may wonder how in the world anyone can do that, be cheerful 24-7, especially in these days of stress and strife. But Paul explained how believers can be constantly content and wholly happy by praying "all the time" and by thanking God "no matter what happens."

Why should you always be cheerful, pray continually, and thank God no matter what happens? Because that's how God wants you to live.

Paul makes the same point again in Ephesians 6:18, telling his readers to "pray at all times as the Holy Spirit leads you to pray. Pray for the things that are needed. You must watch and keep on praying" (NLV). Live and pray as God would have you live and pray.

*Lord, help me to be cheerful, pray
continually, and thank God—no matter what.*

CHEERFULLY EXPECTANT

Don't burn out; keep yourselves fueled and aflame.
Be alert servants of the Master, cheerfully
expectant. Don't quit in hard times; pray all the harder.
ROMANS 12:11–12 MSG

Feeling burned out? Looking for more energy and joy as you walk the walk and talk the talk? If so, it may be time to examine your prayer life.

If you're feeling burned out, you may be working in an area other than the one God has designated for you. If your energy is waning, you may need to spend more time in God's presence praying. If you're running out of patience and feeling overwhelmed with duties, you may need to look around. See if someone else is chomping at the bit to do a duty you're more and more reluctant to perform because your heart is no longer in it.

If your joy in the Lord is waning, change things up by being cheerfully expectant. Before and after you pray, believe with all your heart that God is going to come through for you—big time! Then keep your eyes open as you wait for Him to move on your behalf.

No matter what, Lord, I will stay cheerfully expectant in prayer.
For I know that I find my energy, joy, and strength in You.

GENUINE PRAYERS

GOD can't stand pious poses, but he delights in genuine prayers. . . .
Prayerful answers come from God-loyal people; the wicked
are sewers of abuse. GOD keeps his distance from the wicked;
he closely attends to the prayers of God-loyal people.

PROVERBS 15:8, 28–29 MSG

God knows which of your prayers are genuine. He knows when you're praying with a true and honest heart, one stripped of any pretense. Those prayers, those words, those pleas that you bring before God, the ones that come from the truest of sources, the depth of your being, are the ones that God will closely attend to. As He hears your prayers, God can read the tenor and secrets of your heart.

Today, consider where your prayers might be falling short of authenticity. Look to see where your heart may be leading you and where God's Spirit is guiding you. If those two destinations are not the same, reexamine your heart's desires. Ask God to reveal the discrepancy between His plan for your life and the one you've had at the back of your mind all along.

Lord, I want my prayers to be genuine.
Help me align my path with Yours.

THE SURE THING

We are sure that if we ask anything that He wants us to have, He will hear us. If we are sure He hears us when we ask, we can be sure He will give us what we ask for.

1 JOHN 5:14–15 NLV

. . . .

On a scale of 1 to 10 (1 being the lowest confidence and 10 the highest), how sure are you that if you ask anything of God—anything that's in agreement with His will for you—you'll receive it? To be effective, this question, as with all others, must be answered honestly.

If your confidence in God's coming through for you is less than 7, you may want to consider spending some time building up that confidence and expectation. Why? Because this faith walk you're on may amount to nothing if you don't trust God to act, speak, and deliver in accordance with His Word. If you have no trust in His power, promises, and response to your prayers, you may need to spend more time soaking your spirit and saturating your soul in God's Word, reacquainting yourself with His will, way, wisdom, and wonder.

God, You are the one sure thing in life. Hear my prayer.

IF, THEN

*"If My people who are called by My name put away
their pride and pray, and look for My face, and turn
from their sinful ways, then I will hear from heaven.
I will forgive their sin, and will heal their land."*

2 CHRONICLES 7:14 NLV

God has called you to Him. In response, you have become a follower of Jesus. You are now labeled as a Christian. For you are indeed a believer in the One who sacrificed His life so that you could live forever with God.

As a Christ follower called by God, you must put aside your pride. Put away all your own solutions and answers to questions, puzzles, and problems, and submit to God's wisdom. Look for His way, His motion, His energy in your life. Seek God in all circumstances and in all places. Turn from the pathways of the disingenuous and sinful.

Then and only then will God hear and heed your prayers directed to His heavenly throne. Look for His face as He forgives your sin, as He heals not only you and yours but also your land, giving new life to all that has been destroyed.

*Hear my prayer, Lord, as I put away my pride
and seek Your face and forgiveness.*

→ DATE:

Dear Heavenly Father, ...

....

....

....

....

Thank You for. . . ..

....

....

....

....

....

....

....

....

I am worried about. . . ..

....

....

....

....

....

....

PEOPLE I AM PRAYING FOR TODAY. . . ..

....

....

....

....

....

Here's what's happening in my life. . .

I need. . .

OTHER THINGS ON MY HEART THAT
I NEED TO SHARE WITH YOU, GOD. . .

amen.
Thank You, Father,
for hearing my prayers.

Forgiveness 101

"In prayer there is a connection between what God does and what you do. You can't get forgiveness from God, for instance, without also forgiving others. If you refuse to do your part, you cut yourself off from God's part."
MATTHEW 6:14–15 MSG

· ·

In Matthew 6, Jesus teaches His disciples how to pray. To make it simple, God's Son gives them—and in turn, you—the exact words to pray. And within those words (of what would eventually be known as the Lord's Prayer), Jesus includes the line, "Forgive us our sins as we forgive those who sin against us" (Matthew 6:12 NLV).

Yet when it comes to forgiveness, Jesus doesn't stop there. He makes sure His followers get it straight, that they know exactly what the deal is when it comes to excusing the misdeeds of others. Jesus tells them, "If you forgive people their wrongdoing, your heavenly Father will forgive you as well. *But if you don't forgive people, your Father will not forgive your wrongdoing*" (Matthew 6:14–15 HCSB, emphasis added).

God knew and continues to know His human creatures very, very well. He knows just what to say to get His people on the road to holiness, to heaven, to Him. For He conditions His forgiveness of you on your forgiveness of others. In other words, your acceptance of God's gift of forgiveness for your wrongdoings is a conditional blessing. Through God's grace, He forgives you for all the errors you've made and all the missteps you've taken. And now through the grace God has given you, you can forgive others.

WAY WENDING

*Is anyone among you sick? He should send for the church leaders
and they should pray for him. They should pour oil on him in the
name of the Lord. The prayer given in faith will heal the sick man,
and the Lord will raise him up. If he has sinned, he will be forgiven.*

JAMES 5:14–15 NLV

Prayer is an amazing resource. Whether thought or spoken, your cries, concerns, and confessions wend their way to the ears of the Creator of the world. This Creator, this God and Father of all creatures, listens and takes action as needed, according to His way and will, His plan and purpose. All because you made a decision to cry out, to have faith, to reach out to the invisible Creator of the universe.

Toward the end of his letter to the twelve tribes, the apostle James gives you a wonderful way to tame your tongue. Instead of speaking, pray. When? When you're suffering, pray. When you're feeling cheerful, sing praises toGod. When you're sick, call for the elders and ask them to pray for and anoint you. And if it be God's will, you will be raised up. Physically and spiritually, your sins will be forgiven.

*I cry out to You in faith, Lord. Forgive and
heal me, Lord, within and without.*

FESSING UP

*If we [freely] admit that we have sinned and confess
our sins, He is faithful and just (true to His own nature
and promises) and will forgive our sins [dismiss our
lawlessness] and [continuously] cleanse us from all
unrighteousness [everything not in conformity to
His will in purpose, thought, and action].*

1 JOHN 1:9 AMPC

It can be difficult to fess up to someone things that you've done wrong. That's something a human learns early in life. For when something is amiss and a parent asks a child if he or she knows anything about it, chances are the child will respond with something like, "I don't know. . .but I didn't do it." Although the little one has yet to know her letters or numbers, she somehow instinctively knows enough to say, "I didn't do it"—whether it's true or not.

So it makes sense that you may, at times, have difficulty freely admitting to God all the things you have done, intentionally and unintentionally, outside of His will and way. Yet that's just what you're to do. You're to go to God in prayer and voluntarily let Him know just how many times and ways you've misstepped.

Today, make a clean breast of things to God. You'll be so glad you did!

Dear Lord, I've made some mistakes. . . .

EMPATHETIC UNDERSTANDING

*Try to understand other people. Forgive each
other. If you have something against someone,
forgive him. That is the way the Lord forgave you.*

COLOSSIANS 3:13 NLV

It has been years since the offense against you actually happened.
Yet today, whenever you think about the "incident," you still have that
toxic bitterness of unforgiveness souring not just your heart but your
life! And God knows that's no way to live your life. As someone once
said, "Not forgiving someone is like drinking poison and expecting
the other person to die."

Fortunately, the apostle Paul provides wisdom around forgiveness.
One of the best ways to begin the process (and forgiving someone
can definitely be a process) is to try to understand the person who
offended you, to put yourself in their shoes. Consider their life history and present circumstances. Why might this person have acted
as they did?

Yet even after you've considered the who, what, when, where, and
why of an offense, forgiveness really just comes down to having the
grace, love, mercy, and compassion to simply let go of the bitterness
and thoughts of revenge. That's where prayer comes in. And that's
how prayer saves you.

*Lord, only You can help me let go of my
unforgiveness. Help me to do that, right here, right now.*

LETTING GO

If your brother sins (misses the mark), solemnly tell him so and reprove him, and if he repents (feels sorry for having sinned), forgive him. And even if he sins against you seven times in a day, and turns to you seven times and says, I repent [I am sorry], you must forgive him (give up resentment and consider the offense as recalled and annulled).

LUKE 17:3–4 AMPC

Biblical scholars say that according to Judaism, forgiving someone three times (Job 33:29–30; Amos 1:3; 2:6) was enough to demonstrate your forgiving spirit. But when Peter asked Jesus how many times he must forgive a fellow believer, asking, "As many as seven times?" (Matthew 18:21 ESV), Jesus responded, "I tell you, not seven times but seventy times seven!" (Matthew 18:22 NLV). Seventy times seven is 490 times!

That's a lot of forgiveness! And the only way you can actually do it, to meet the bar Jesus has set, is to get closer and closer to Him. To sink yourself and your spirit deep into His words. To spend so much time with Jesus that you too, if necessary, can forgive anyone anything. And not just forgive but give up the resentment you may be holding on to. Woman, just let go and let God.

Help me, Lord, to let go of any lingering resentment against anyone. In Jesus' name.

BY THE CURB

Put out of your life all these things: bad feelings about
other people, anger, temper, loud talk, bad talk which
hurts other people, and bad feelings which hurt other
people. You must be kind to each other. Think of the other
person. Forgive other people just as God forgave you.

EPHESIANS 4:31–32 NLV

All of God's children are works in progress. That's why the Bible is filled with ways in which you can become less of a flesh follower and more of a Spirit follower.

In his letter to the Ephesians, the apostle Paul advised believers to become better God followers by filling a receptacle with all the garbage you might still have in your life. Topping the list is "all bitterness, anger and wrath" (verse 31 HCSB). To that barrel of trash you can add "loud talk, bad talk which hurts other people, and bad feelings which hurt other people." Basically, God wants you to be kind, loving, and forgiving to *all* people. And that includes yourself.

Today, consider embracing Paul's advice. Leave your trashy behavior, attitudes, and actions by the curb and then embrace the new you.

Lord, help me be the woman You want me to be, one who is
kind, loving, and forgiving to others. . .and to myself.

→ DATE:

Dear Heavenly Father, ...

....

....

....

....

Thank You for. . ...

....

....

....

....

....

....

....

I am worried about. . ...

....

....

....

....

....

....

PEOPLE I AM PRAYING FOR TODAY. . ...

....

....

....

....

....

Here's what's happening in my life. . .

I need. . .

OTHER THINGS ON MY HEART THAT
I NEED TO SHARE WITH YOU, GOD. . .

amen.
Thank You, Father,
for hearing my prayers.

Cultivating Thankfulness

Let the peace of Christ keep you in tune with each other,
in step with each other. None of this going off and doing
your own thing. And cultivate thankfulness.
COLOSSIANS 3:15 MSG

. . . .

Although words and phrases like *please* and *thank you* tend to be rarely used in an increasingly impolite society, they are an integral part of your relationship with God.

In prayer, *please* implies you're approaching God with heartfelt respect and humility. You, the petitioner/worshipper, are acknowledging that *God* is the One who holds all power, strength, and wisdom. *He* is the One who is deserving of your gratitude.

And the phrase *thank you*, when truly felt and expressed, is a reward not just for the one receiving the thanks but also for the one expressing the thanks. At the end of a thank-you-and-you're-welcome exchange, both parties are warmly lifted up.

In his letter to the Colossians, the apostle Paul made it clear that the lives and mouths of believers "should be full of thanks" to God (Colossians 2:7 NLV). That you should not only keep praying and stay alert in prayer but "be thankful always" (Colossians 4:2 NLV).

Over the next five days, you'll be exploring the role and effect of having an attitude of gratitude and using it to cultivate thankfulness. Because everything God has created is good. "And nothing is to be rejected if it is received with thanksgiving, for it is made holy by the word of God and prayer" (1 Timothy 4:4–5 ESV).

GIVE THANKS

*Give thanks to God—he is good and his love never
quits. Say, "Save us, Savior God, round us up and get
us out of these godless places, so we can give thanks to
your holy Name, and bask in your life of praise."*

1 CHRONICLES 16:34–35 MSG

If you really sit and think about it, hopefully you will find that many people do many things for you. Yet when others touch your life with kindness by opening a door for you, picking up lettuce on the way home, or covering for you when you're sick, you may not even take notice of it. Or you may feel it's too menial a favor to actually acknowledge the act with a thank-you.

Perhaps it's time to open up your eyes to the goodness and kindness of others. To acknowledge the acts of kindness done for you. To say thank you. To everyone, regardless of age, creed, color, nationality, and political party. It's time to appreciate one and all.

Today, be alert. Open your eyes, ears, and mind to the acts of kindness happening all around you, encouraging and inspiring you to give thanks for all you have and are in God.

*Thank You, Lord, for never giving up on me.
Thank You for all Your blessings and mercies.*

GOD, THE ENRICHER

The One who provides seed for the sower and bread for food
will provide and multiply your seed and increase the harvest
of your righteousness. You will be enriched in every way for all
generosity, which produces thanksgiving to God through us.

2 CORINTHIANS 9:10–11 HCSB

Imagine you're at a restaurant and your server comes to your table with several plates filled with the delicious food you've ordered. As he begins setting the platters before you, chances are a "thank you" is going to pass your lips. But will you utter another "thank You" to God as well?

It's easy to take your friends, family, and Father God, as well as their kind actions, for granted. But doing so can be dangerous, even hazardous to your health. Studies have found that expressing gratefulness and counting blessings can improve your sleep, lower your stress, and enhance your relationships with others!

Today, consider thanking God for all He does for you, all He provides for you. Recognize what He has given to you so that you can be a fount of blessing, a source of encouragement to someone else.

All I am and have is from Your hand, Lord. Thank You
for being so generous, so loving, so wonderful.

SEVEN THANK-YOUS

Give thanks to the Lord for His loving-kindness and His great works to the children of men! For He fills the thirsty soul. And He fills the hungry soul with good things.

PSALM 107:8–9 NLV

Psalm 107 begins with its author telling you to "give thanks to the Lord for He is good!" Then the psalmist proceeds to tell you *why* you should be thanking God. For His goodness, of course. Then for His loving-kindness and His deliverance of you. Also for redeeming and setting you free, filling your hungry soul with good things, leading you, bringing you out of darkness and into His life, breaking your chains, and so on.

Woman, God has done and continues to do so much for you day after day after day. So today, be sure to thank Him. In fact, make gratitude a daily practice, for it will not only increase your prayer power but lift your heart, soul, spirit, and mind.

Perhaps consider listing seven things each day that you're thankful for. Split the list so that you can get your mind in a good place at the very beginning of your day and ease your mind at the end of the day. Start now!

Good morning, Lord. Thank You for. . .

THE PASSWORD TO GOD'S PRESENCE

Applaud GOD! Bring a gift of laughter, sing yourselves into his presence. . . . He made us; we didn't make him. We're his people, his well-tended sheep. Enter with the password: "Thank you!" Make yourselves at home, talking praise. Thank him. Worship him.

PSALM 100:1–4 MSG

What an amazing concept! Not just that you can be so bold as to enter God's presence and spend time with Him. That in itself is amazing. But what seems so absolutely astonishing is that the way to get there, the password to enter into His court of praise, is the phrase "Thank You"!

Psalm 100 is a short song, only five verses total. Yet it seems to cover everything. It's all about being joyful when you call out to God. Being glad while you serve God, coming into His presence with a song on your lips. Then knowing that He, God, is the One who is the Creator, the boss, the worker of miracles. He made you. You are one of His people, one of the sheep in His pasture of peace and promise.

Today, do as the psalmist advises. Enter into God's presence with a joyful song in your heart and "Thank You" on your lips.

I've got the password, Lord! THANK YOU for everything!

WHATEVER YOU DO

Whatever you do, in word or in deed, do everything in the name of the Lord Jesus, giving thanks to God the Father through Him.

COLOSSIANS 3:17 HCSB

God has a purpose and a plan for you. He knows your entire story, all the good and the bad. He has you here, now, for a reason. As you walk the earth with Him, He is with you every step of your journey. He is the One going before you, walking with you, and serving as your rear guard. He is your GPS, the One who whispers advice, telling you which paths to take.

Yet God knows the difference between a heart that is truly thankful and one that is only paying lip service. If you're not quite there yet, one way to obtain a truly thankful heart is to do all things not just in the name of Jesus but also "in [dependence upon] His Person, giving praise to God the Father through Him" (Colossians 3:17 AMPC).

Today and every day, depend on Jesus to help you, no matter what you're doing in word or deed.

Lord, today, help me do all things in Your name and through Your power and strength, wisdom and wonder

→ DATE:

Dear Heavenly Father, ...
....
....
....
....

Thank You for. . . ..
....
....
....
....
....
....
....
....
....

I am worried about. . . ..
....
....
....
....
....
....

PEOPLE I AM PRAYING FOR TODAY. . . ..
....
....
....
....
....

Here's what's happening in my life. . .
....
....
....
....

I need. . .
....
....
....
....
....
....
....
....
....
....
....
....
....
....
....

OTHER THINGS ON MY HEART THAT
I NEED TO SHARE WITH YOU, GOD. . .

....
....
....
....
....
....
....
....

amen.
Thank You, Father,
for hearing my prayers.

God the Provider

I have [your full payment] and more; I have everything
I need and am amply supplied. . . . And my God will
liberally supply (fill to the full) your every need.
PHILIPPIANS 4:18–19 AMPC

. . . .

Psalm 23 is the best known of all psalms. And its first verse says it all: "The Lord is my Shepherd [to feed, guide, and shield me], I shall not lack" (AMPC).

Because you are a believer, God is your Shepherd, the One who leads you to still waters, urges you to rest in quiet pastures, and provides you with abundant food. God, your provider, has got you covered, meeting all your needs, not just today but every day. Thus, because God is in your life, you shall never lack anything. Ever. This truth is something you need to write on your heart, emblazon across your mind, and sear on your soul. Woman, you have everything you need. Right here, right now. And God will continue to supply you with what you need—and more—into eternity!

God wants you to accept His unending provision as truth. For as soon as you do, as soon as you are assured He will meet your every need, you can focus your time and energy on abiding in His will and way. Not just today or in this moment but every day and in every moment. For your God is "generous to a fault," lavishing His "favor on all creatures" (Psalm 145:16 MSG).

PAST PROVISIONS

*GOD, your God, has blessed you in everything you have done.
He has guarded you in your travels through this immense
wilderness. For forty years now, GOD, your God, has been
right here with you. You haven't lacked one thing.*

DEUTERONOMY 2:7 MSG

Enslaved in Egypt for centuries, the Israelites cried out to God. Hearing their groans and remembering His covenant with Abraham, God began taking steps to prompt Pharaoh to let His people go. First, He met with Moses via a burning bush. Then He enlisted Aaron to help Moses. Ten plagues later, God was escorting His people out of Egypt, through the Red Sea, and into the wilderness.

Then, for forty years, God journeyed with His people, protecting them, guiding them, and providing for them. For forty years, their shoes and clothing never wore out (Deuteronomy 8:4; 29:5). When His children complained they had no food, He provided manna from heaven (Exodus 16:15). When they needed water, God provided it out of a rock (Exodus 17:6).

The point is, God always provided for His people in the past. And He will do so for you in the present. You can count on it—and Him!

*Thank You, Lord, for always being there for
me. With You, I lack not one thing!*

EXPECTANT PROVISIONS

*The Lord upholds all those [of His own] who are falling
and raises up all those who are bowed down. The eyes
of all wait for You [looking, watching, and expecting]
and You give them their food in due season. You open
Your hand and satisfy every living thing with favor.*

PSALM 145:14–16 AMPC

Your Lord and Savior is not just a great provider—He is *the* Great Provider. When you don't know where your next paycheck is coming from or how you'll find a way to pay the rent or mortgage, don't panic. Stay calm. Rest easy. For God is there for you. He, the Lord and Creator of all, will take care of you.

The thing is, when you leave all your needs in God's hands, confident that He will indeed uphold you and provide just what you need when you need it, God is *certain* to come through for you. For "He Himself gives everyone life and breath and all things" (Acts 17:25 HCSB).

Today, put yourself and your hope in God's care, knowing you *will* receive all you need from His open hand.

*Lord, I expectantly look to You alone for all I need.
Thank You for taking such great care of me! Amen.*

PROMISE OF PROVISIONS

*The Lord is near to all who call on Him, to all who
call on Him in truth. He will fill the desire of those who
fear Him. He will also hear their cry and will save
them. The Lord takes care of all who love Him.*

PSALM 145:18–20 NLV

When words of prayer, praise, and petition pass your lips, God hears them. For He listens to all who pray to Him, to every person who calls His name and speaks to Him with words of truth. Even if you technically cannot speak in words, God knows what you mean to say. He knows what you're thinking, experiencing, living through. And He's got you covered.

God has promised, over and over again, that He is here for you. That's His part. Your part is to believe He is actually there, listening for and then aiming to fulfill your needs and desires.

Even after the first two humans—Adam and Eve—went against His instructions not to eat the fruit of the tree of knowledge, God still provided for them, many times without them even crying out. God knew what they had need of before they did themselves! (See Genesis 3:21 and 9:3.)

*Thank You, Lord, for always meeting my needs—
even before I know them myself!*

213

CAREFREE

*"There is far more to your inner life than the food you
put in your stomach, more to your outer appearance than
the clothes you hang on your body. Look at the ravens,
free and unfettered, not tied down to a job description,
carefree in the care of God. And you count far more."*

LUKE 12:23–24 MSG

To help people understand how important they are to God, Jesus urged them not to be so concerned about their needs in the material world. For their lives were so much more than the food they ate or the clothes they put on their back. Today He's giving you that same message.

No matter how many years have passed since Jesus walked the earth in the flesh, you have the same basic needs as the people who lived all those years ago. To live, you need food, water, air, clothing, and shelter. You need someone to love you, lead you, help you.

The wonder is that God fits and fills all those requirements, providing you with not just what you need to survive but what you need to thrive!

Today, live "carefree in the care of God" by leaving your needs and desires in His hands, knowing He will lovingly fill them and more.

Lord, show me how to live carefree in Your care.

A SAFE PLACE

Strong people will honor You. . . . For You have been a strong-place for those who could not help themselves and for those in need because of much trouble. You have been a safe place from the storm and a shadow from the heat.

ISAIAH 25:3–4 NLV

Let's face it. There may be some things you aren't able to do for yourself. There may be times when you need someone to come alongside to be your guard, defense, protector. Look no further. For the Lord of the Universe, the King of the cosmos, the Creator of all creation is here. And all you need to do is cry out, call on His name, pray to let Him know what's going on, where you are, what you need. And He will come through for you.

When trouble hounds your heels, go to God, your strong place. He will keep you hidden from view. He will put a hedge of protection around you that no one and no power can breach. If things are getting too hot to handle, allow and expect God to shadow you from the intense heat.

Woman, there is no shame in reaching out to a higher power to help you stand when you cannot stand on your own. God is here to be your strength. Let Him. And you will prevail.

Lord, be my safe place and stronghold.

215

→ DATE:

Dear Heavenly Father, ...
....
....
....
....

Thank You for. . ...
....
....
....
....
....
....
....
....

I am worried about. . ...
....
....
....
....
....
....

PEOPLE I AM PRAYING FOR TODAY. . ...
....
....
....
....
....

Here's what's happening in my life. . . ..

....

....

....

....

I need. . . ..

....

....

....

....

....

....

....

....

....

....

....

....

....

....

....

OTHER THINGS ON MY HEART THAT
I NEED TO SHARE WITH YOU, GOD. . .

....

....

....

....

....

....

....

....

amen.
Thank You, Father,
for hearing my prayers.

Comfort through the Spirit and Prayer

Our God. . .gives us comfort in all our troubles.
Then we can comfort other people who have the same
troubles. We give the same kind of comfort God gives us.
2 CORINTHIANS 1:3–4 NLV

When trouble comes knocking at your door and you find yourself in need of comfort, logic may lead you to seek the solace of others who have gone down the road you're now on. But Jesus has left you an even better resource.

When Jesus was readying His followers for His departure, giving them last-minute advice, direction, and wisdom, He told them He would ask God to give them another "Comforter (Counselor, Helper, Intercessor, Advocate, Strengthener, and Standby), that He may remain with you forever—the Spirit of Truth" (John 14:16–17 AMPC).

That Comforter Jesus was talking about is the Holy Spirit. And that Spirit is the One who resides in you now! The Spirit will teach you all you need to know and lead you to that prayed-for peace (and pluck) you seek.

When trouble strikes, pray. Ask the Comforter to hold you, hide you, and help you. To give you the strength and confidence, the wisdom and help, the succor and truth you need so you can find courage and calm. And when, at some point, you get back on your feet, become a comforter yourself, for others. Just as God designed you to do.

218

COMFORT AND JOY

*"I will comfort you as one is comforted by his mother. And you
will be comforted. . . ." When you see this, your heart will be
glad. Your bones will get new strength like the new grass. And
the hand of the Lord will be made known to His servants.*

ISAIAH 66:13–14 NLV

. . . .

God promises He will be with you in troubled times. He will comfort
you just as well as (if not better than) any good earthly mother would
comfort her newborn baby. Imagine such a baby, one who finds her
complete comfort, as well as her joy, contentment, and nutrition, in
the arms of her mother. For a baby, there is no better place to rest,
recover, and be renewed.

Just as that mother is there to comfort her baby, God is there
to comfort you. As Isaiah says, "The Lord will always lead you. He
will meet the needs of your soul in the dry times and give strength
to your body. You will be like a garden that has enough water, like a
well of water that never dries up" (Isaiah 58:11 NLV).

Today as you pray, ask God to help you ingrain upon your mind
that God, your Comforter, is waiting with arms wide open. Come.

*Lord, I come to You today, in this moment. Hold me
close and fill me with Your comfort. I'll rise in joy!*

COMFORT, LIGHT, AND LORD

*Be strong, courageous, and firm. . . . It is the Lord Who goes
before you; He will [march] with you; He will not fail you
or let you go or forsake you; [let there be no cowardice or
flinching, but] fear not, neither become broken [in spirit—
depressed, dismayed, and unnerved with alarm].*

DEUTERONOMY 31:7–8 AMPC

When your strength is sapped, your courage weak, and your determination dodgy, pray to God, the maker and mover of heaven and earth, who goes before you. He is your forever scout, the One who will always give you signs that you're heading in the right direction. He will keep you on the safe path by warning you of the dangers ahead and by leading you away from the quicksand, over the mountains, and into God country—the land of prayer and promises.

As much as God is your scout, going before you, He is also the friend walking at your side and the guard at your rear. And He always will be. He promises never to leave you.

Today as you pray, feel God before, beside, and behind you. Thank Him for always being there.

God of all, You, surrounding me, are my comfort, my light, my Lord.

A COMFORTING SHEPHERD

*The Lord is my Shepherd. . . . Yes, though I walk
through the [deep, sunless] valley of the shadow of death,
I will fear or dread no evil, for You are with me; Your rod
[to protect] and Your staff [to guide], they comfort me.*

PSALM 23:1, 4 AMPC

. . . .

When you're walking amid long shadows in a deep valley, the experience can be a bit intimidating. For you never know who or what lurks within the depths of the darkness. But if God is your Shepherd, leading, feeding, and sheltering you, you can take comfort in the fact that you'll be safe. No matter where you are.

When you're stuck in a gloomy place and need help extricating yourself from it, remember your Good Shepherd. He holds a rod of protection to defend you from anyone moving to harm you or to put you in harm's way. And along with that rod of protection, the Shepherd carries a staff to guide you one direction or another. There may be times when He uses that same rod and staff to bring you back when you're drifting away or need correction.

God is prepared to keep you safe and sound. Are you ready to let Him?

Good Shepherd, comfort me as we walk this path.

221

NEITHER SHAKEN NOR STIRRED

*God is our safe place and our strength. He is always our
help when we are in trouble. So we will not be afraid,
even if the earth is shaken and the mountains fall into
the center of the sea, and even if its waters go wild with
storm and the mountains shake with its action.*

PSALM 46:1–3 NLV

"Mother Earth" seems displeased with her caretakers these days.
Each year, the weather seems to be more and more severe. Forests
are aflame, mountains tumbling, glaciers melting, earthquakes rumbling, hurricanes hurling, and seas rising. It's enough to keep you
from stepping outside some days.

How the earth got into this state is one thing. How you're going to
navigate its effects on your life is another. But God wants you to know
that no matter what happens in your life, no matter what situation
you face, He is the One you're to run to for safety and strength. He
is always there to help you when trouble is on the horizon.

God has you and those you love in His hands. Call on Him, run
to Him, and kneel in stillness before Him (Psalm 46:10).

*Because of You, Lord, I'm neither
shaken nor stirred. Simply still. . .in You.*

LIFT UP

*I will lift up my hands to Your Word, which I love, and
I will think about Your Law. Remember Your Word to Your
servant, for You have given me hope. Your Word has given
me new life. This is my comfort in my suffering.*

PSALM 119:48–50 NLV

Might as well face it. Some days will be difficult at best, for life is not always easy. Yet even then God can be your comfort. For even on those hard days, God keeps His promises. He promises to be with you through thick and thin, pain and gain, life and death, good and bad. You are simply to lift up your hands and praise God on good days and bad.

Today and every day, remember God's Word, your love of it, your need of it. Dig into it, looking for His promises, His voice, His guidance. Allow Him and His Word to plant a seed of hope to lift you up. Let that seed give you new life, new strength, new insight, new outlook.

Today, open up your spirit, soul, mind, and heart to God. Permit His Word to be your healing balm, your comfort, your new song.

*Lord, give me hope and new life through the
wonder of Your Word. Lift me up!*

→ DATE:

Dear Heavenly Father, ...
....
....
....
....

Thank You for. . ...
....
....
....
....
....
....
....
....

I am worried about. . ...
....
....
....
....
....
....

PEOPLE I AM PRAYING FOR TODAY. . ...
....
....
....
....
....

Here's what's happening in my life. . .

I need. . .

OTHER THINGS ON MY HEART THAT
I NEED TO SHARE WITH YOU, GOD. . .

amen.
Thank You, Father,
for hearing my prayers.

From "Our Father" to "Amen"

*Pray at all times (on every occasion, in every season) in the Spirit,
with all [manner of] prayer and entreaty. . . . Amen! (So be it!)*
EPHESIANS 6:18; REVELATION 7:12 AMPC

- -

When you first encountered God, you may have envisioned Him as a
sort of father figure. But then, as time passed, you began to see Him
as more than a father. The more you got to know Him, understand
Him, the more you began to see Him as a friend, shepherd, guide,
and protector. For in the lives of His people, God has played many
roles. As A. W. Tozer said, "Always, everywhere God is present, and
always He seeks to discover Himself to each one."

Yet when Jesus taught His followers how to pray, He began what
became known as the "Lord's Prayer" with the words "Our Father"
(Matthew 6:9). Jesus may have chosen this title as a hint to His disciples that He, the Eternal Son of Father God, would, by His actions,
open a channel so that all who accepted Him would, along with Him,
be considered sons and daughters of God themselves!

You, woman, are a daughter of God. He, your Father, has promised
to provide for you, love you, care for you, protect you, and draw you
closer to Him, who is in heaven, eagerly awaiting your prayer, from
"Our Father" to "Amen."

PRAYER AND PERSPECTIVE

Caleb. . .said, "Let us go up at once and take the land. . . ."
But the men who had gone up with him said, "We are not able
to go against the people. They are too strong for us."
NUMBERS 13:30–31 NLV

Twelve spies had been sent by Moses into the wilderness to scope out the Promised Land. When they returned, ten of the spies said the land was indeed one full of milk and honey. "But the people who dwell there are strong, and the cities are fortified and very large" (Numbers 13:28 AMPC). In fact, the people the ten spies saw from their man-to-man perspective were *so* large that they claimed, "We were in our own sight as grasshoppers, and so we were in their sight" (Numbers 13:33 AMPC).

Fortunately, two of the spies, Caleb and Joshua, had a completely different take on the power of God versus the strength of the people inhabiting the Promised Land. With God, they'd be victorious!

When fear and panic come into your life, pray for a new perspective, for God's point of view. And you too will enter a land of promise.

Lord, change my perspective. Give me a brighter outlook!

PRAYER AND "OUR FATHER"

"This is your Father you are dealing with, and he knows better than you what you need. With a God like this loving you, you can pray very simply. Like this: Our Father in heaven, reveal who you are. Set the world right; do what's best—as above, so below."

MATTHEW 6:8–10 MSG

. . . .

Abba God, your supernatural Daddy, knows exactly what you need and when you need it. So your prayer life doesn't have to be complicated. That's why Jesus gave you an example you can follow, a pattern you can use to come to Father God with your problems, praises, and petitions.

And what's wonderful in the wording of *The Message* is the idea that you don't always have to begin your prayer with "Our Father." Instead, why not consider how God has been revealing Himself to you or, perhaps even better, consider how you might want Him to reveal Himself to you right now?

For God is all things to you. Right now you might need a protector or provider more than you need a father figure. Or perhaps you'd like to see God as Light and Love. In these last pages of your Prayer Map, consider using a different address for God your Father, and record where that takes you.

Lord, our Father. . .Lord, my Guide, hear my prayer. . . .

PRAYER AND PEACE

Do not worry. Learn to pray about everything. Give thanks to God as you ask Him for what you need. The peace of God is much greater than the human mind can understand. This peace will keep your hearts and minds through Christ Jesus.

PHILIPPIANS 4:6–7 NLV

The great mitigator of panic and mayhem, of chaos and confusion, of worry and doubt, is a vibrant prayer life. That's why you're advised to pray. About what? Everything! And while you're there, in front of God the Father, give Him thanks as you're asking for what you need!

Then praise God. Why? Because that's not just how you'll get through life but how you'll succeed! And by "succeed," increased financial or material wealth is not what is meant but rather an increased understanding, godliness, and Christlike character!

Today, see God from a peace-giving and peace-loving perspective. Acknowledge that He is your only avenue to calm in this world. As you lean more and more on God and less and less on your own strength, the more God's peace will guard your heart and mind. What a God you serve!

"May [our] peace-giving God be with you all! Amen (so be it)" (Romans 15:33 AMPC).

PRAYER AND THE AMEN

These are the words of the Amen, the trusty and faithful and true
Witness, the Origin and Beginning and Author of God's creation:
I know your [record of] works and what you are doing.

REVELATION 3:14–15 AMPC

. . . .

Jesus. He's the Amen. The One described as the Witness, the Origin, the Beginning and Author of God's creation. He knows your entire life record of works, past, present, and future. Jesus is called the Amen because He is the source of all truth. Jesus speaks what He knows and tells us exactly what He's seen. The truth begins and ends with Him and the words coming from His lips and landing in His Book of Truth.

The phrase "in Jesus' name, amen" tacked onto the end of prayers has been uttered so often it has almost lost its true meaning and strength. Yet Jesus did instruct His followers to ask "in My Name [as presenting all that I Am]; but now ask and keep on asking and you will receive, so that your joy (gladness, delight) may be full and complete" (John 16:24 AMPC). And He also instructs you to end your prayers with "amen," which means "so be it," confident God will hear and make your request a reality.

Lord Jesus, hear my prayer prayed in Your name. . . . So be it!

OPEN DOOR

These are the words of the Amen. . . . Behold, I stand at the door and knock; if anyone hears and listens to and heeds My voice and opens the door, I will come in to him and will eat with him, and he [will eat] with Me.

REVELATION 3:14, 20 AMPC

Jesus, the Amen, is standing and knocking at the closed door of your heart. It's not that He's seeking shelter from the storms of life. After all, He has power over all storms—within and without! No, He wants to come in. To live with you, abide in you, break bread with you, and just plain be with you. He loves you so deeply but cannot be a part of your life unless you open the door and allow Him to enter, for the handle to the door is only on your side.

Today, listen closely for Jesus' knock. Is there some part of your heart that is not yet open to Him and His will and way? If so, consider opening yourself up to Jesus. Allow Him to enter in, to become a part of your life, to partake of your ups and downs, ins and outs. Resolve to begin and end in Him.

Jesus, I open my door to You, Your love, Your Spirit, Your Father. Let's eat!

→ DATE:

Dear Heavenly Father, ...

....

....

....

....

Thank You for. . . ..

....

....

....

....

....

....

....

....

I am worried about. . . ..

....

....

....

....

....

PEOPLE I AM PRAYING FOR TODAY. . . ..

....

....

....

....

....

Here's what's happening in my life. . .

I need. . .

OTHER THINGS ON MY HEART THAT
I NEED TO SHARE WITH YOU, GOD. . .

Amen.
Thank You, Father,
for hearing my prayers.

SCRIPTURE INDEX

OLD TESTAMENT

NEW TESTAMENT

THE PRAYER MAP FOR THE ENTIRE FAMILY. . .

The Prayer Map for Men
978-1-64352-438-2

The Prayer Map for Girls
978-1-68322-559-1

The Prayer Map for Teens
978-1-68322-556-0

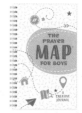

The Prayer Map for Women
978-1-68322-557-7

The Prayer Map for Boys
978-1-68322-558-4

These purposeful prayer journals are a fun and creative way to more fully experience the power of prayer. Each page guides you to write out thoughts, ideas, and lists. . .which then creates a specific "map" for you to follow as you talk to God. Each map includes a spot to record the date so you can look back on your prayers and see how God has worked in your life. *The Prayer Map* not only will encourage you to spend time talking with God about the things that matter most, but also will help you build a healthy spiritual habit of continual prayer for life!

Spiral Bound